2021

LOOKING

INTO

THE FUTURE

Betsey Lewis

2021 Looking into The Future by Betsey Lewis

© 2020 by Betsey Lewis. All rights reserved. (1)

ISBN: 978-1070674896
Library of Congress Cataloging-in-Publication data

Cover design by Betsey Lewis

Book Titles by Betsey Lewis
Extraterrestrial Encounters of The Extraordinary Kind
2020 Prophecies and Predictions
Star Beings
Déjà vu
Ancient Serpent Gods
Mystic Revelations of Seven
Mystic Revelations of Thirteen
Prophecy 2016 and Beyond: The Prophets Speak
Earth Energy: Return to Ancient Wisdom
Communicating with the Other Side
Angels, Aliens and Prophecy II

Spiritual Books for Children
Alexander Phoenix
The Story of Rainbow Eyes
A Worm Named Sherm

CONTENTS

ACKNOWLEDGEMENT

Thank you to all the people who submitted questions for this book!

This book is dedicated to my loving Spirit Guides and my Indigenous mentors, Oglala Sioux Ceremonial Leader and Author Ed McGaa "Eagle Man," and Spiritual Leader of the Western Shoshone Nation Corbin Harney (1920-2007), who opened my eyes to the natural and unseen world around us.

PREFACE

Note: Today is November 11, 2020. Biden and all the news media proclaim him our new United States President, yet there's still uncounted votes and the issue of voter fraud in several states. When I began this book, it was August of this year, and events have drastically changed since the November 3 election. In September, I had a powerful vision of Trump winning as I had foreseen seven months before the 2016 election. The die has not been cast yet as Trump's attorneys seek to file lawsuits in Federal Court on ballot fraud. According to many sources and those who will testify in court, fraud was massive across the country. This is not how democracy works—this is a coup by the Biden group to take over our country without a final vote decision. The media does not have the power to call an election.

The Bible's Book of Proverbs says *Fools rush in where Angels fear to tread.* The proverb means that rash people who attempt extreme things that more experienced people would avoid. That's me. All my life I've done things that people have told me that I couldn't or shouldn't do, but I did it despite their warnings.

A dark cloud has descended on America and it's racing around the world to cover the entire globe if we don't act fast. We were warned by prophets and psychics that such a day was coming, but we failed to believe it and did nothing to stop it, and perhaps we couldn't even if we tried.

Writing this 2021 prediction book has been deeply troubling to me because I know that those who speak out against the tyranny will be silenced as they have already been. It is with a heavy heart that I write this book as election events unfold. On November 7, 2020, a seven-power number day, I sensed the Family of Dark was going to declare Biden president and they did with 279 electoral votes to Trumps 213. The date 11-78-2020, totals 13, the Illuminati number (refer to my book *Revelations of Thirteen*).

All major networks declared Biden/Harris victorious!

But they had no right to do declare anything. How could Trump go from winning the election to losing in several states within hours where massive ballots appeared magically in Biden's favor? This has not been a fair election—this feels more like a coup and tyranny against the American citizens and President Trump.

In a press conference recently, attorney and former New York City mayor, Rudy Giuliani introduced several people who weren't afraid to come forward and describe how they witnessed election ballot fraud taking place. There are states still counting votes and awaiting military ballots. How can the election be over?

In a vision, I saw a dark cloud enshrouding America, but I will hold on to a glimmer of hope until the last minute that I was given a God-given vision of Trump's destiny. I hope all of you reading my book will feel the same. It's not over until it's over. I knew that Biden was corrupt, but this proves how corrupt he really is—a wolf in sheep's clothing, and masses of people bought into his deceit.

What bothers me are the sheeple that voted for Biden. Joe Biden's daughter wrote in her diary that he had her take showers with him, and she told her therapist that she had been molested but didn't say by whom. She has battled drug addiction like her brother Hunter Biden who has been involved in child pornography, human trafficking, and money corruption in Ukraine according to several sources. There's also a photograph of him in a bathtub and asleep with a crack pipe in his mouth.

They say the apple doesn't fall far from the tree and it's true. Like father, like son. Both his daughter Ashley and his son Hunter went through drug rehab, and Ashely said her father had her take showers with him. Her diary hinted at molestation but didn't give a name. Ashley's full diary is available on the internet.

I've seen it before in families where there is molestation. How could people vote for such an immoral man and a deceitful man? There are plenty of videos on YouTube of Biden whispering in little girl's ears and sniffing their hair. The man has some real issues!

Many psychics like myself and prophets were given visions of President Trump being reelected. Evangelist Pat Robertson had a vision of him winning and global apostolic leader Pastor Robert Henderson received four lucid dreams about President Donald J. Trump's destiny for America and winning the election. The preacher and prophet Kim Clement had a vision in 2007 of a man named Trump who had a major destiny in America. He said that he would have two terms. Kim Clement died in 2016 before Trump was elected. There are articles on the internet claiming at least ten psychics predicted his win. How could we all get it wrong? Because fraud, deceit, and corruption stepped in and may have altered destiny. The fight isn't over.

There is a reconning coming to our Planet. It's out of balance physically, mentally, politically, and spiritually. We will have to wait and see how events play out now. Will the Family of Light win or will the Family of Dark succeed to control us? It's going to be a fight—a spiritual fight that has been fought over the centuries.

We still have a choice, but we will have to fight hard for it. Don't use violence, but words and make them count. Stand up for your beliefs of democracy and don't let those ignorant intimidate you.

For a long time, our reality has been engineered into a frequency and pattern of a downward spiral into the darker and heavier energies that are at the lower end of the scale in which the human body can exist. This was not a plan conceived on a moment's notice. It is one that has been put together over eons of time. It is one that has been put together over eons of time. However, because their plans are counter to creation and God, we can upend their final plans for control.

You are probably wondering how this rebellion was allowed to continue to this point? The freewill aspect is what has been exploited as the basis for their ability to manipulate humanity to be the vehicle of their power. They know that humanity is malleable enough to be influenced and controlled. Mass mind-control through television, cell phones, advertising, social media. They tell you what you want to hear and will never make it happen.

We can change the vibratory pattern. However, the Family of Dark has worked out ways to create this downward vibration into heavier energy rather than lifting of vibration as was intended. They seek the darker entities that surround our world and delve into satanic rituals they have used for centuries. This control happens when the mass consciousness of that vibratory level of planetary experience has its focus on experiences at the lowest level of our reality.

Here's the good news. There is a point at which their restrictive pressure of controlling the thought processes of the mass consciousness of the planet can backfire and cause exactly the opposite of what they have planned. This will cause them to panic and run for their lives. It's more involved, but I won't go into that at this time—perhaps in a later book.

They are so confident that their dark agenda will succeed, they forget about the *Butterfly in the Hurricane*, where many souls come together in thought and prayer and created a sudden mass change in consciousness worldwide.

We have been admonished by a time traveler named John Titor who appeared in a blog in the year 2000, claiming he was from the year 2036, only sixteen years from now. He claimed that timelines can change and had changed each time he time jumped. John was asked if some sort of new world government was in place by 2011. And John's response was, "On my worldline, in 2011, the United States is in the middle of a civil war that has dramatic effects on most of the Western governments."

It seems that America is on the verge of a second Civil War. He said the civil war was started by politicians, but he should have included our news media. John referred to our current society and seemed to see our world as beyond help when he stated, "Have you considered that your society might be better off if half of you were dead? While you sit by and watch your Constitution being torn away from you, you willfully eat poisoned food, buy manufactured products no one needs, and turn an uncaring eye away from millions of people suffering and dying all around you. Is this the 'Universal Law' you subscribe to?"

John said this about our future and our society when he said,

"Perhaps I should let you all in on a little secret. No one likes you in the future. This time is looked at as being full of lazy, self-centered, civically ignorant sheep. Perhaps you should be less concerned about me and more concerned about that."

Whoever John Titor was, he was right about the humans we have become. The world I grew up in was totally different and people were kinder. There were bullies, but not like today. The internet has given these bullies a mouthpiece to be cruel and hateful.

This is not a time to hide and use your usual excuse of "What can one person do." A large number of "one persons" can accomplish a great deal. Using violence and guns is not the way to do it. Subtle energy is powerful, and the most powerful energy is subtle. The Bible says, "In the beginning was the word." But words are thoughts spoken out loud. In the beginning was pure thought!

Simple change the focus of your thought. Do know dwell on hate and upon the horrors of the agenda planned for humanity but turn your thought to what it is that you would like to experience on this planet at this time.

It seems that the destiny of the planet has been wrestled from the control of its citizens, and the Republic of the United States of America has been taken over in a coup. How long do you think it will take people to rise up and say, "I'm mad as hell, and I won't take this anymore?" It's coming. Just look at the world and how opposed humans are to the control of wearing masks due to the Coronavirus pandemic. We don't like barriers and control.

Again, I will speak out against the media and their lies and sensational negative news. We are addicted to TV, cell phones, movies, and soul jarring music, all lower vibrations. These vibrations infiltrate your brain—and now we have 5-g cell towers.

We often turn over our power to religious entities, but we are the power. We have always had the power but have allowed it to be taken from his through though control.

Perhaps if Biden does become the President, and I am right, we are in for some very dark times. Perhaps it is our lesson to awaken and stop giving away this innate power we have. It will be an extremely difficult lesson for those of us who know the truth, but as the Bible says, *"Ye will know the Truth, and it will set your free."*

Think about those powerful words. You need only to open your eyes, consider the changes in your personal freedoms that are being removed from your world in succession. What if the internet suddenly went down and there was no cell phone service? What would you do? You'd rely on your instincts, your intuition, and intellect to survive like the ancient people.

Freewill is our birthright and a God-given gift. We stand at a critical junction in our world. It's time to rewrite the script where the bad guys win, and the hero dies. Our movies have programmed us that evil never dies and lives on. It can't be destroyed. These scenarios were enacted in real life during several wars—Korea, Vietnam, and Desert Storm. It was a no-win situation, unlike World War II where we defeated Japan and Nazi Germany.

We have been given rewritten histories that future generations will never question about events and our leaders. They will read articles or watch YouTube that these were only conspiracy theories like 9-11 and that John F. Kennedy's assassination was by a lone gunman named Oswald. If it's written in a history book for children, it must be true, right? Wrong! That's how communist countries mold their children to be obedient adults. The Light of the world, future generations, and they must be told the truth that they can pass on to their children. Native people believe that what we do will affect the next seven generations. We have a major responsibility to these children about the truth, one that isn't homogenized for control!

Your soul decided to return to this specific era to be a *System Buster* and make positive changes. Don't fear the Earth changes coming, the Family of Dark and other events coming. They will pass and someday you and I will be long gone and perhaps forgotten thousands of years in the future when we will return to new bodies and heal and balance the planet. But I'll guarantee that you will be honored as a *System Buster*.

Our planet is our spaceship. It looks very fragile from here, and it's very easy to take it for granted when we're living on it when it seems so big and so massive. But it's not. It's very small and very fragile. —NASA Astronaut Sandra Magnus in 2009

ONE
THE WAY WE WERE

Indigenous people worldwide have foreseen the coming changes for many decades and have warned us to prepare for a new Earth. They tell us we must return to the natural way of living as Earthkeepers, as they have practiced as the ancient ancestors did for thousands of years. Once we do, our planet will return to balance or *ayni.*

The Maya, the Hopi, and Inca all speak of the purification time when Earth will turn or flip on its axis. Andean prophecy foretells of a coming period of transformation, when the Condor and the Eagle align, and a time of cosmic overturning of time and space that will signal the end of an era. During the time of purification, many will choose to leave, and those who remain will find new ways to exist. The new children born during this time are old souls who are reincarnating very quickly, sensing they have an important role in the coming Earth changes. These children bring a higher frequency with them and enhanced psychic gifts—for they have been altered by *The Watchers* of our world, and they are the newly evolved human.

Will humanity finally stop their silly dogmas and superstitious beliefs that have controlled our way of life for thousands of years? It's time to awaken from our deep slumber.

Will we ever embrace the teachings of the Masters who have walked upon Earth long ago? They taught us to love, to honor one another, and to live in peace and harmony with each other and the planet. Those Master also spoke of moving mountains with our minds and that we could heal and do other words as they did. But we don't believe anymore that such power is possible for mere mortals.

Growing up in the 1960s and rural Southern Idaho was a special time for me, and if a time machine existed, and I'd go back to that time period in a heartbeat. People were kinder, the sky was bluer, and lakes, rivers and the ocean were cleaner not like in today's world. When I think about the little children of the world today, my heart is filled with sadness for the future generations who will live in an uncertain world full of prejudice, hate, violence, and perhaps anarchy.

Those of you who have read my *2020 Prophecies and Predictions* know that I began having premonitions as a young child. I have experienced countless paranormal events and have been shown the future through dreams and visions. Sometimes I feel as if my gift is a curse because I don't like giving bad news to my readers.

Although I don't recall my invisible friend, my mother recalled my two angels or perhaps extraterrestrials that gave me "secret messages" at the age of three. I didn't recall what messages were given, but I sensed all would be revealed as an adult. And they were!

When I turned seven-years-old, a huge silver disc followed me home from my first-grade elementary school in Twin Falls, Idaho. The walk should have taken fifteen minutes, but instead, I arrived 45 minutes to one hour late. My mom was worried.

Shortly after the UFO encounter, catastrophic earth changes filled my dreams each night for a week. It was like viewing a television screen except I was experiencing the events in real-time where I was transported to different locations around the world. There were powerful earthquakes as I escaped on foot with a group of adults as volcanoes erupted, and then the next minute I was transported to an ocean setting and watching a huge tsunami wave rolling in. The really strange part was I wasn't a child in the dreams—I was an adult.

Numbers of people, like me, recall their abductions and were given apocalyptic warnings from extraterrestrials about Earth.

Friends and family, now passed, come back to remind me that they live on. At times, my telekinetic powers allow me to move objects. Streetlights often turn off and rows of lights blink out in department stores and grocery stores when I pass under them. Electronics malfunction all the time.

People ask how I receive my premonitions and visions. It varies. Sometimes I foresee an event, like remote viewing, and sometimes a lucid or symbolic dream is revealed to me. Many times, I experience "the knowing" where I am certain something is going to happen or sense something about a person. Often my sweet Spirit Guides whisper in my ears about future events. Also, they have called out my name early in the morning when they'd awaken me from a sound sleep. It is a bit annoying, but I am accustomed to it now.

Through the years I have experienced premonitions, dreams, and visions warning of major world events before they happen. Weeks before Mount St. Helens violently erupted on May 18, 1980, I had a lucid dream of a volcano's side bulging and then exploding. My father dreamed that Hawaii's Goddess Pele appeared to him and warned him about Mount St. Helens' eruption. This is the only time I recall his premonition gift, but Mom was incredibly psychic. She recalled a past life as an elderly Chinese laborer who helped to build The Great Wall of China and died there. The body was entombed in the rock wall, a fact that was verified years later through discoveries of human remains inside the wall. Mom also had the ability to astral project to different locations.

Some of my premonitions are frightening. In 1968 while living in Los Angeles I was shown an old gypsy woman holding my right palm. She spoke several words as she cut a deep cross into my right palm, causing it to bleed. The dream was symbolic and made little sense at time until leader Martin Luther King was assassinated on April 5, 1968, and later Senator Robert Kennedy was shot after midnight on June 5, 1968, at the Ambassador Hotel in Los Angeles by Sirhan Sirhan, and died the next day. I lived a few blocks from The Ambassador Hotel on Wilshire Boulevard.

The symbolism of my dream was about death and someone famous martyred for his death—both Martin Luther King and Robert Kennedy. We all suffered from President John F. Kennedy's death in 1963, but Robert Kennedy's death, five years later, shattered the Nation for another Kennedy president.

Two years later, one of the reporters at CBS News station in Los Angeles where I worked at the time, was in the lady's restroom with me after doing a special report on Robert Kennedy's assassination. I told her that I felt Sirhan Sirhan was not a lone shooter, and she looked at me in shock and said, "I was at the Ambassador Hotel that night standing close to Bobby, and watched a man come up behind him and shoot him point-blank while everyone was jumping on Sirhan."

I asked why she didn't come forward and tell the authorities about this other shooter. She shook her head and said, "Remember how many people died under strange circumstances who witnessed Kennedy's assassination in Dallas in 1963 and reported a shooter hiding in the grassy knoll?"

I agreed that she was wise to keep silent.

In 1966, I was given a tour of the Beverly Hills house owned by music producer Terry Melcher, actress Doris Day's son located at 10050 Cielo Drive. Lead singer of Paul Revere and the Raiders pop/rock band Mark Lindsay was staying at the home with Melcher and actress Candice Bergen at the time. During the school year in L.A. I met a student who knew Mark Lindsay, originally from Idaho, who I had met at my parent's Lake resort in the Snake River Canyon near Twin Falls, Idaho.

The day I was given the tour by the property caretaker, Charles, I learned that Mark and Terry were out of town. The burgundy-colored house appeared small from the outside. The moment I stepped inside a cold chill permeated my body. The shades were drawn, making the rooms feel foreboding—something evil was going to happen here.

My sister and I returned to Idaho by the summer of '66, but our parents were still fighting. By late '67, I left Idaho with my mom on a Greyhound bus headed to Los Angeles with only one suitcase and one-hundred dollars. Without jobs and a place to stay, we trusted fate to guide us. A kindly man and his wife helped us find employment at Union Bank in downtown Los Angeles and offered their home to us for a few weeks until we could find an apartment.

Two years later there was breaking news about the horrific murders of Sharon Tate and her friends at the Cielo house where Mark Lindsay and Terry Melcher once occupied. The night of August 8–9, 1969, four members of the Manson Family invaded the home of actress Sharon Tate, wife of film director Roman Polanski, under the direction of cult leader Charles Manson. Members of Manson murdered Sharon Tate, her unborn child, hairstylist Jay Sebring, friend Wojciech Frykowsky, and coffee heiress Abigail Folger shortly after midnight. Steven Parent, 18, was only visiting the caretaker at the residence and was shot dead in his car. All the victims except Steven Parent had been stabbed numerous times.

A year earlier Dennis Wilson, a member of the Beach Boys, had introduced Terry Melcher, Doris Day's son, to ex-con and aspiring musician Charles Manson. They all met at Melcher's house, but Melcher declined to sign Manson and his music. Theories suggested Manson believed record producer Melcher still lived at the Cielo house and he was the intended victim, not Tate and her friends.

Somehow, my premonition of that house in 1966 during a tour of Cielo home was uncannily true. Even before Sharon Tate bought the house, the area was rumored to be haunted. People have felt a dark presence in the hillside area. The original Cielo house was demolished in 1994 because of the horrors that took place there. Rumors persist that Sharon Tate's ghost haunts the cul-de-sac road leading up to the top of the hill where her house once stood.

What happened to The Age of Aquarius?

When the moon is in the Seventh House
And Jupiter aligns with Mars
Then peace will guide the planets
And love will steer the stars—This is the dawning of the Age of
Aquarius

When 1968 arrived, my friend Gary and I attended the Broadway play "Hair" at the Aquarius Theatre on 6230 Sunset Boulevard in Hollywood where a giant psychedelic mural was displayed on the building. It was a time that seemed hopeful and that peace would guide humanity in the future. A bright new world was coming, and the Age of Aquarius was going to transform all of us into peaceful, loving humans.

Boy, I was naïve!

While we were living our lives, raising families, going to work from 9 to 5, the world changed, and not in a good way. The internet made it possible for us to instantly connect with others, to get instant news, but like all things in our duality world, there's always a negative side to the positive. Instant news meant mind control and taking away more of your freedom. It was a way to alter our minds and to allow bullies of every age to berate and criticize everything on social media.

A Planetary Revolution is taking place with the Family of Light against the Family of Dark. They say for the next 2000 years we will be in the Aquarian Age after transitioning from the Pisces Age. Some believe we entered the Aquarian Age on December 21, 2012; others believe we entered it on November 11, 2011. We were told that every person would be affected by the shift in consciousness. But that didn't take place as foreseen.

Supposedly the Piscean Age was dominated by hierarchy and power, but it was also about belief and faith. Aquarius is about "I know." This is the age of instant information, computers, cell phones, and advanced technology, where humans seldom interact with each other in person, and especially now that the COVID-19 pandemic has sent us into our homes and distancing each other.

Aquarius is about freedom and independence.

All these years we could have changed our world, but instead of evolving spiritually, most have devolved. We seem to have grown angrier, less tolerant, more judgmental, and bigoted, and less compassionate toward our fellow humans. This period of change and transition coming in the next few years will be trying for everyone, and especially for those who refuse to bend in the wind like a reed.

2021 will bring potential growth and expansion for some, and for others, it will be a time of fear, great pain, and suffering. The more you fight something, the more it persists. If you embrace the coming changes and do it with peace and love in your heart, the easier the transformation will be. Those who fight it with anger, hate, and violence, will find the road ahead extremely difficult.

Jupiter left Sagittarius and moved into Capricorn in December 2019, just before we learned about the Coronavirus being released from a biological laboratory in China. Things have been seething under the surface for a long time and Pluto has been moving slowly, pulling up stuff from the past 12 years, and will remain in Capricorn for another three years from 2020 to 2023.

I foresee a time of cleansing, riots, and four waves of the Coronavirus. Everything that has been put off or hidden will become out and become transparent. Those who hid the truth from the world can no longer keep their secrets, secret. When things fall apart, that means something better is coming. It's the darkest before the dawn.

We will see amazing changes in the coming years with civil rights, environmental consciousness, women's rights, gay rights, and global consciousness. What we do to one another also affects the entire world because we are ONE. For some of you, this is a challenging concept to grasp, but we are One Mind and our thoughts, our actions, and our words alter the world each moment. We are creating our reality.

We will see the rise of terrorism, continue partisan politics, racism, xenophobia (the fear of the "other" person), and general fearmongering, especially in our major news. We have already seen increased divorces, suicides, depression, anxiety, stress, and increased use of drugs, both pharmaceutical and recreational, and alcohol since COVID hit. Humans are always looking for escape and denial, but this is not the time to go into your cave.

We came into this world to be "System Busters" and that means we chose to be here at this time to bring forth a bright new world. We should speak our peace but not force others to adhere to our beliefs. Those who refuse to listen will awaken in time. The Shift happening will bring out the best and worst in mankind. We have already witnessed the heroes, the ones who are selfless and put others first—they will advance faster in the spiritual world.

Some people are preparing for this shift, both a physical one and a spiritual one. Some will open their hearts and minds and embrace the new age, and others will fear the changes. Transformation is never an easy process. In these times, it is important to have a clear mind and a healthy body. Everyone on this planet will experience the shift in consciousness and perhaps the shift of Earth's poles as Edgar Cayce and other prophets was foreseen., which I was shown in recurring dreams at the age of seven. We are indeed headed for transformational change.

Practice some sort of spiritual tradition whether it be meditation, prayer, or through your religious beliefs.

Did you know that Aquarius stands for revolution? That's exactly what we are experiencing now.

The sun in Pisces, and Mercury retrograde in Pisces, was hiding the reality of the situation about the pandemic. All the facts were hidden from us at first by the Trump administration because they did not want us to panic. Guess what—we did panic! Everyone ran to the grocery stores and bought everything in sight and left shelves bare. People hoarded toilet paper and soon there was none to be found for weeks. I watched in horror as people ran into grocery stores and stole whatever they could, and no one could stop them. It was madness.

Whether or not you want to condemn or honor Trump for his decisions early in the pandemic, we'll never know what another leader might have done unless they were in Trump's shoes. The world had not seen a pandemic s in over 100 years since the Spanish Flu hit worldwide from 1917 to 1919. Trump, however, did shut down the borders from Chinese entering the United States. Even though he was warned it was bad, no one knew how bad it was going to get, not even the health experts like Dr. Fauci. Trump realized that people would panic—and he was right!

We like to play the blame game and never take the

responsibility for ourselves. Doctors told us how deadly the virus was and that we should protect ourselves, but a huge percentage of people did not want to believe it was that deadly and many still believe it's a conspiracy. Perhaps some of their beliefs are correct.

I find it beyond coincidence that COVID appeared the year of the U.S. election, and how easily Biden was able to convince the public (most anyway) in repetitious ads that it was Trump's fault with his election donation dollars in the millions.

Saturn is still in Pisces and leaves on December 17, 2020, and it asks us to make sure that we know the consequences and reality of the situation we have gotten ourselves into as a species. Are we going to act on what needs to change in our society?

We have forgotten how to be the Family of Light. You will be challenged to redefine what is light and what is dark, good, and evil. As the Family of Light, we are here to create a frequency of healing and balance around Earth, to take the highest opportunity possible, the most difficult task of raising the frequency from one of anger, violence, despair and fear to one of joy, ecstasy, love, and self-power. Once this happens, humans will have changed the frequency of control, and experience the thousand years of peace that has been prophesied.

Some believe a Messiah, or beings from benevolent realms will solve our problems and give us the solutions to the pandemic, wars, and pollution. Now we await the metamorphosis of consciousness.

In the years to come, a great play of Nature will take place, as our Mother Earth will view for our attention. She is going to rage and she's asking for our attention that "Change is Here." Remember that many events will seem real but are holographic. There is no need to become frightened of the changes coming to our world, although fear, fright, and hell on Earth will be expounded and sold by religions and the news media. Those who have been controlling humans for eons, know us, and how easily we are mind-controlled. People also forget events and the truth behind them such as what happened on September 11, 2001. We were told that three buildings were destroyed by airplanes when only one was hit. Building two was videoed and showed a plane didn't hit it as the alter videos were shown on every network news station. The videos showed us over and over two planes hitting each building, except building 7, that was never hit, yet collapsed. Smoke and mirrors, my friends, and the "controllers" know that humans are easily hoodwinked.

The Hopi people have the sacred Prophecy Rock in Northern Arizona that depicts two roads we can travel. The higher road guides you to God (Everlasting Life) and the lower road leads you to destruction. The Hopi say this story has repeated itself many times for as far back as human memory reaches, and they have predicted where we will end up if we don't change course immediately. Three previous human worlds were destroyed when the people became greedy, worshiped technology as a god, fought and hurt each other, and repeatedly forgot the ethical teachings they'd been given to honor the Earth as the source of life and sustenance. Three apocalypses inevitably ensued—first by fire, then by ice, then a flood. Noah's Ark floated through one book's collective memory to escape a similar greed-ending catastrophe. The future is visible in the now.

We are at the crossroads of decision. It is at this point that destiny of each human is set. Humans have free will to choose the Guided Path or not. The rock also depicts three gourd rattles symbolic of three world wars. It is after the third war; a Golden Age begins.

The second world-shaking would be recognized when man used the Hopi migration symbol (swastika) in war.

The third world-shaking would be recognized by a red cover or cloak. (Prophecy Rock below)

The question confronting creative, spiritual people today is: How are we going to emerge on the other side of this earth-transforming moment in history? Again, I ask, what kind of world do you want for the child being born now? Do you want them to hate us for not awakening to the tyranny and control taking place on our planet? Will they see us in this timeline as hateful, vindictive, violence, and mind-controlled, civically ignorant sheep as time traveler John Titor said?

2021 Looking into The Future

CHAPTER TWO

PRESIDENT DONALD TRUMP

I am ashamed to call the United State my home, and it's not because I don't love America, it's because I have never in my entire life seen people behave in such a vile way and how they have treated the Presidency of the United States and President Trump. No president has ever been treated so unfairly and berated by the press, media, and others. It's as if humans have become possessed and the evildoers (George W. Bush's expression) want to take over the world, but there will be a reckoning…and soon.

Trump isn't perfect and he has made mistakes as president, but he is the far better choice than Joe Biden. Although Biden said he would wait until all votes were counted, he lied and took the role before all the votes were counted. He now projects himself as the 46th President of the United States to the world and has reached out to leaders worldwide. This election is far from over because not all votes have been counted, including military votes in many states, and fraud took place in several states according to witnesses who watched ballot tampering.

Although I had a vision of Trump winning the election, I didn't factor in deceit and blatant fraud of our democracy as a free nation. This is what happens to communist countries that rig their polls. Our voices don't seem to count in Biden's world. Is this the New America?

As they say, it isn't over, until it's over. If our country has become this corrupt, there must be tentacles of corruption everywhere and Trump won't have a chance to reclaim a victory. He was ahead in the polls at the beginning and it was huge and then suddenly everything changed where thousands of ballots were added with Biden's name.

Those who voted for Biden will later regret that vote if he really does become the President-elect, and not by the news media. The saddest part is your Biden vote will hurt all of us in a new socialist America. My tears fall as I think about the evil that has been planned for humanity for the last twenty years, and the Family of Dark didn't even have to force you to buy into their evil. You bought it—hook, line, and sinker—you were deceived.

As of September 2020, President Donald Trump has been blamed for the 200,000 plus souls who have died due to the Coronavirus pandemic in the United States since February. Biden said that if he was president at the beginning of COVID, he would have been truthful to the American people about the deadly virus and he could have saved lives.

We will never know what Biden would have done if he was president when the pandemic struck the United States. It is always easy to judge another person unless you have walked in their shoes. Trump did shut down the borders from China and as he has stated he probably did save lives.

Can you imagine the soul-searching President Donald Trump had to face even when he was told that the virus was different from any flu ever known on this planet? Even doctors and scientists didn't know how virulent Coronavirus was unleashed on the world from a biological laboratory in China. The release of this biological weapon was long planned by the New World Order to destabilize our world.

If Biden becomes our next president, he will be unable to do anything about the next three waves of the virus. He will be as chastised and condemned as Trump was. Those who touted him will eat crow as his dementia or Alzheimer's Disease becomes worse.

I foresee a time where Biden as President (if he does stay elected) will be removed due to his progressed disease or die in office before 2024, and that means Kamala Harris will become President, and God helps us if that happens.

A little over one hundred years ago, the Spanish Flu raged worldwide. Some say it started in 1918, but there is evidence that deaths began in Europe by late 1917. The flu infected 500 million people—that's about a third of the world's population at the time, and it hit in four successive waves. Estimates of deaths range from 17 million to as many as 100 million, making it one of the deadliest pandemics in human history.

I find it odd the virus struck at the beginning of 2020 as the election campaign was getting in full swing.

Remember Trump feared people would panic, and people eventually did panic, rushing to the grocery stores and buying everything on the shelves. People across the United States began hoarding food—toilet paper, meat, and everything they could get their hands on. Grocery stores shelves were bare for weeks. Trump was right! And lest we forget, toilet paper became as scarce as hen's teeth for weeks.

In 2016, seven months before the election, I predicted on my website, on Facebook and Twitter, that Donald Trump would become our 45th President as I had seen in a powerful vision where he was taking the Oath as President in a dark overcoat and Melania was in a light-colored outfit. The prediction happened as I had foreseen. Newsmax included my prediction of Trump's 2016 win in their on-line article on Nov. 5, 2016. https://www.newsmax.com/Headline/Psychics-divided-Election/2016/11/05/id/757228/

Trump came into this life to drain the swamp as he called it—dirty politicians.

Recently right-wing Pastor Robert Henderson had four prophetic dreams that began in 2016 about President Donald J. Trump. He said that Donald Trump cannot be removed because He is 'God's Choice,' and that the 'Courts of Heaven' elected him. Pastor Henderson has been shown that Trump has a destiny and will win the election.

In the first dream, Henderson claimed to have received a phone call from Trump during the Republican presidential primaries in 2016 in which Trump asked him to hold a conference in support of his campaign. Henderson said that he held that conference on July

6, 2016, and that it helped Trump secure the Republican nomination.

After Trump won the election, Henderson claims to have had a second dream in which Trump asked him to be a part of his Cabinet, which Henderson interpreted as meaning that he was to be Trump's representative in "the courts of Heaven" and "stand in the council of the Lord on behalf of his administration."

Following Trump's inauguration, Henderson claims to have received yet another dream call from Trump, this time asking him to serve as Trump's running mate in 2020. "I knew he wasn't asking me to be his vice president," Henderson said. "But I knew that God was asking me to run in the spirit with him. So that is what I have been doing for the last three-plus years, running in the spirit with him."

Henderson wasn't the only person to have a vision of Trump's win for November 3, 2020. Evangelist Pat Robertson said God told him Trump will win. He also claimed to have seen a vision of an asteroid hitting Earth in five years.

How could our vision be wrong? Though Trump's people are well aware of the Family of Dark's plans and massive election fraud sting in process. Will these crimes be brought to justice in the public eye? That depends on the justices and even the Supreme court and if they will stop this tyranny. People are taking to Twitter and other social media that a coup is taking place by the socialists of the United States. One woman wrote, "They have tried to steal this election in a Venezuelan-style fashion to implement socialism in America."

Angry people are already gathering around the country to protest the coup and showing up at polls and talking to city officials that they witnessed ballots being destroyed or other voter fraud.

So, I will reiterate, I see foresee Trump being re-elected, and this will cause the left to riot, burn, and loot cities again. Did you notice that none of Trump's did anything after Biden was declared the next President?

2021 Looking into The Future

2021 Looking into The Future

CHAPTER THREE

JOE BIDEN AND KAMALA HARRIS

The news media took it upon themselves on Saturday, November 7, 2020, to declare Joe Biden the winner of the presidential 2020 election, even though the votes had not been counted in each state, and election corruption was becoming blatantly obvious in many states. How audacious of them! Why is Biden being pushed as our President-elect? What happened to democracy and fair elections? We are watching our constitution being ripped from us and we feel utterly helpless. But there is light at the end of the tunnel.

President Trump's attorney Sidney Powell has gone on Fox News to declare they have evidence of multiple states involved in voter fraud, and lawsuits are being prepared as I write this.

How could the nation be so comatose to vote for Joe Biden and not see his real agenda behind his words?

Joe Biden is poised to unleash a series of executive actions on his first day in the Oval Office, prompting what is likely to be a year's long effort to unwind President Trump's domestic agenda and immediately signal a wholesale shift in the United States' place in the world. Does he plan to expunge Trump from our history books?

Joe Biden will be 78 years old on November 20, 2020, He continues to show increasing dementia during his rallies. He recently introduced his granddaughter as his dead son Beau Biden at a rally.

Already Biden is showing the early stages of Alzheimer's disease—mental decline, difficulty thinking and understanding, confusion in the evening hours, delusion, disorientation, forgetfulness, making things up, mental confusion, difficulty concentrating, inability to create new memories, inability to do simple math, or inability to recognize common things. Behavior can include—aggression, agitation, difficulty with self-care, irritability, meaningless repetition of own words, personality changes, restlessness, lack of restraint, or wandering and getting lost (Biden often forgets the State that he is visiting). His mood can change from anger, apathy, general discontent, loneliness, or mood swings. Joe Biden often becomes angry when asked certain questions during his interviews.

October became a month of shocking revelations about Joe Biden and his son Hunter Biden's illegal operations in Ukraine, yet the new media tried to cover it up and never mention it.

Explicit photographs and emails were found on a laptop belonging to Hunter Biden and posted on the internet. The story first broke with the New York Post. According to Trump's attorney, Rudy Giuliani, his laptop photographs showed Hunter involved in child pornography and asleep with a crack pipe in his mouth.

Trump is drug and alcohol-free and the same goes for his children, unlike both Joe Biden's son Hunter and his daughter Ashley were involved in drugs.

Joe Biden during the debate with Donald Trump on October 22, claimed that his Ukraine accusations came from Russia. Without a shred of evidence to disprove the New York Post's Hunter Biden story, the mainstream media and Democrat lawmakers quickly reverted to their tired playbook of "Russia, Russia, Russia."

Reporter Drew Holden presented a comprehensive thread of screenshots of mainstream media reporters from CNN, *The New York Times*, NPR, PBS, CBS News, MSNBC, *The Washington Post, USA Today,* and even Business Insider all parroting the same talking point of "Russian disinformation," without evidence to support it.

From the beginning, Hunter Biden's position on the board of a Ukrainian energy company was "awkward" and "problematic" at the time his father, Joe Biden, was serving as vice president, two

Republican-led Senate committees said in a recent report. Joe Biden was secretly playing footsie with China.

In a statement on Oct. 21, it asserted that the former vice president was a willing participant in a family scheme to make millions of dollars by partnering with a corrupt Chinese Communist firm. The explosive assertion is believable because it aligns with earlier information known to be true provided by Tony Bobulinski, the former business partner of Hunter Biden, who describes Joe Biden and Joe's brother Jim in the China scheme.

Bobulinski confirmed that he was of the recipients of the May 13, 2017 email published by The New York Post. The email, from another partner in the group, laid out cash and equity positions and mysteriously included a 10 percent set-aside for "the big guy," believed to have referenced his father, Joe Biden. The claims go against everything Joe Biden has ever said about Hunter's many businesses and Joe's knowledge of them. He has flatly lied to the American people.

After all, Joe and Hunter traveled together to China on Air Force Two, where Hunter landed a $1.5 billion commitment from a government-controlled Chinese bank. Then there was Hunter's $83,000-a-month gig on the board of a Ukrainian energy company—despite his lack of experience in Ukraine or knowledge of energy. Do you think it's a coincidence that Joe Biden was vice president for the Obama administration's point man in both countries? It seemed that wherever Joe went, Hunter followed. As they say, the apple doesn't fall far from the tree. There were similarly lucrative deals in Russia, Romania and Kazakhstan — that we know of.

Did you know this about the Obama/Biden administration? On Jan. 17, 2016, the day after four American detainees, including The Washington Post's Jason Rezaian, were released, a jumbo jet carrying $400 million in euros, Swiss francs and other currencies landed in Tehran, Iran. That money purportedly was partial payment of an outstanding claim by Iran for U.S. military equipment that was never delivered. Soon after, $1.3 billion in cash followed. In 2018, President Trump tweeted this, "Never gotten over the fact that Obama was able to send $1.7 billion in cash to

Iran and nobody in Congress, the FBI or Justice called for an investigation."

Supposedly that incredible amount of money in cash given to Iran was a legal settlement that the United States owed Iran from before the 1979 revolution. Really? With that cash, Iran turned around and developed nuclear weapons.

Iran is not a member of the Missile Technology Control Regime (MTCR) and is actively working to acquire, develop, and deploy a broad range of ballistic missiles and space launch capabilities. Iran used ballistic missiles in attacks on target in Syria's Civil War and has proliferated missiles to its non-state allies in the Middle East. They launched a coordinated ballistic missile strike against the United States assets in Iraq on January 2, 2020, in response to the U.S. assassination of the high-ranking Iranian commander Soleimani.

We can assume some of the cash Iran was given by President Obama and V.P. Biden was used to develop nuclear weapons. Iran is also a sleeping giant. I foresee conflagrations between Iran, Syria, and the United State in 2021.

During the first debate on September 29, 2020, with Joe Biden and President Trump, Biden claimed he wanted to send $20 billion dollars to Brazil to save the rainforests. Biden said that if elected president, his administration would rejoin the Paris Agreement and rally wealthy nations to protect Brazil's rainforest as part of a greater effort to combat climate change. Brazil's President Jair Bolsonaro was angered by Joe Biden's suggestion that Brazil could suffer economic consequences if it does not stop Amazon deforestation, calling it a "shame" and "a sign of contempt."

"What some have not yet understood is that Brazil has changed," Bolsonaro, a close ally of President Donald Trump, wrote on social media. "Its President, unlike the left-wing presidents of the past, does not accept bribes, criminal land demarcations, or coward threats towards our territorial and economic integrity."

In the mid-1990s, I had the opportunity to visit the rainforests of Belize and spend two weeks in the jungles at a shrimp farm and a jaguar reserve. I observed acres of rainforest being clear cut and burned for farmers to plant their orange groves. That's how this third world country survives. I was saddened by the destruction of the precious life-given forests there and how thousands of animals, insects, and medicinal plants are destroyed.

Major wildfires globally have destroyed thousands and thousands of acres of land, homes, and lives in the Western United States, Australia, and Brazil. Has global warming created drought conditions throughout the world or is geoengineering to blame?

This September 2020 is recording accelerated deforestation in part of the Pantanal area—a vast wetland known as the cradle for endangered species in western Brazil. During the first two weeks of September, over 5,000 heat points (fires) were recorded in the Pantanal biome, the most for that period since 2007. So far in 2020, the number of fires in Brazil is 208% higher than in 2019, according to Brazil's Spatial Research Institute.

Trees provide oxygen for the Earth and without trees, all life on this planet would die. In one year, a mature tree will absorb more than 48 pounds of carbon dioxide from the atmosphere and release oxygen in exchange.

As my mentor and friend, Corbin Harney (1920-2007), Spiritual Leader of the Western Shoshone Nature, said, "As I see it all around me, the trees are dying out, our water is contaminated, and our air is not good to breathe. Those are the reasons why today I am trying my best to come back to our ways of thousands of years ago. We have to come back to the Native way of life. The Native way is to pray for everything. Our Mother Earth is very important. We can't just misuse her and think she's going to continue."

Joe Biden told a Las Vegas, Nevada reporter at KTNV-TV on October 9 that voters, "don't deserve" to know his position on whether he would seek to expand the number of justices serving on the Supreme Court if elected. So far Joe has not answered the question for reporters or during the two debates. The limit has always been nine Supreme Court Justices.

During the debate on Thursday, Oct. 22, 2020, Joe Biden claimed that he never said he would eliminate fracking and "end fossil fuel", and Trump said he could prove that he said that from recent clips. Biden dared Trump to put any evidence had made about anti-fracking statements on his Twitter account, and Trump did on Twitter. Biden lied.

I am an environmentalist, but we can't return to our dependence on foreign oil and gas again. That's what Biden would do. It will take time to wean ourselves off oil and gas and find alternative forms of energy that won't harm our environment. It would be a disaster to stop oil and gas drilling and fracking in this country. Millions of jobs would be lost. Already 58 million people have filed for unemployment since the beginning of the pandemic.

September 2020, California's Democratic Governor Gavin Newsom announced that he will aggressively move the state further away from its reliance on climate change-causing fossil fuels while retaining and creating jobs and spurring economic growth—he issued an executive order requiring sales of all new passenger vehicles to be zero-emission by 2035 and additional measures to eliminate harmful emissions from the transportation sector.

It will be interesting to see how fast car manufacturers move to electric cars and will there be enough stations to charge our cars by 2035?

If I am wrong about Trump winning and Joe Biden does not become the 46th President and Kamala Harris as the Vice President, I foresee a dangerous road ahead for America. At this moment, the 2nd wave of Coronavirus is hitting across the United States and hospital overwhelmed by the sick in some states like Utah and Idaho. New York is again repeating a huge spike as hospitals fill in New York City.

If a lockdown happens, there will be more business closing, huge unemployment for the masses, homes repossessed, and great numbers of people homeless and moneyless, seeking food and shelter for their families.

The people who voted for Biden will become disenchanted with his changes, and eventually, they will want him removed from office—perhaps impeached. I see Biden will no longer occupy the Presidential seat either because of his dementia or his inability to run the country, death, or an assassination. It is not clear at this time. That means Kamala Harris will become the President. Her background as an attorney and US Senator since 2016, does not give her the background to become President of the United States. She served as District Attorney in San Francisco from 2004 to 2011. However, I don't foresee her as President—ever!

Clyde Lewis (no relation), the host of Ground Zero late-night talk show, wrote this in his monologue on November 9, 2020.

Around the time we called out Dark Winter, long before Joe Biden acknowledged it – that plan was underway for a psychological operation that both political parties were aware of and Donald Trump confirmed there would be a viable vaccine by Election Day. However, as we reported Friday, there was a tabletop asymmetrical warfare exercise that was carried out six months ago where a fictitious election between Joe Biden and Donald Trump would wind up with Biden beating Trump with a called electoral vote.

The war game plan was carried out by the Transition Integrity Project. The scenario predicted a narrow Biden victory in the Electoral College: 278 to 260. The group that represented Team Trump was told not to concede the election under no circumstances. They were told that they had to use whatever means necessary to secure the 10 electoral college votes to swing the election. They were asked to focus on three of the swing states that in this particular scenario Biden had gained— Michigan, Wisconsin, and Pennsylvania because, in all three, Republicans control both branches of the legislature. Normally, the governor certifies the election results, and in all three states, the governor is a Democrat. But there is nothing to prevent the legislature from certifying a different election outcome.

In the mock transition scenario, the Republican Party bombarded the airwaves with claims of electoral fraud and insisted that Trump had been cheated of victory. The GOP filed suit to prevent the certification of the results. Attorney General William P. Barr supported this effort in this mock exercise by claiming to have detected efforts by Chinese intelligence, Antifa terrorists, and other enemies of the people to steal the election. While this was going on, chaos reigned in the streets, with pro and anti-Trump activists mobilizing massive protests and violence erupting. Democrats believed that mass protests could force the government to respect the election outcome. But the team representing Trump calculated that such chaos would help persuade the Supreme Court to intervene to shut down the dispute. In 2000, even two of the more moderate conservative justices—Sandra Day O'Connor and

Anthony M. Kennedy voted to end Florida's recount between Al Gore and George W. Bush and hand the election to Bush.

The question is—was it all that fictitious or was it part of a psychological operation and has it gone real-time under the auspices of *Dark Winter*?

It would appear that a mock exercise has gone real world and that a massive psy-op is now being offered and the media and the people are being led into it without a doubt because of the new found feelings of unity that we are told the country is feeling.

The goal was to tie up the proceedings in the courts, initially at the state level, and quickly force the Republican-dominated Supreme Court to intervene.

If the Transition Integrity Project has gone real world, then this is a massive psy-op that has been launched across the world because no one is even thinking that the existing and forthcoming litigation from the Trump team might change the final tally in key battleground states, and in turn influence how the Electoral College votes in the middle of next month, since it's this institution – not the media or the popular vote – which legally decides the presidency, as per the Constitution.

With the psy-op reaching its crescendo towards what might ultimately end up being Trump's official capitulation (although no such concession on his side is constitutionally required), the question on his supporters' minds is whether or not they should recognize the contentious results even if the Electoral College certifies them. That's a personal decision that every person must make for themselves, though it should be said that everyone should abide by the law and not burn, loot, riot, and even murder in rare instances like the "deep state's" de-facto street militias of Antifa and "Black Lives Matter" have done for nearly the past half-year with practical impunity when expressing their rage against the system. Nevertheless, consent is purely personal and doesn't have to be given even if one goes through the motions of abiding by the certified outcome to avoid the possible consequences of being placed on the "enemies list" that some of the dictatorial Democrats are currently compiling.

Of course, the enemies list was not part of the mock exercise, but it was to be expected—*Dark Winter* means so many things to the Deep State operatives that are behind it. After we reported that the election would be in favor of Joe Biden as per the exercise there were a few other things that were also in play and that was how COVID-19 would also be used to create even more mistrust of the people as there would be talk of an overnight miracle cure or vaccine that would certainly tune the tide for the election.

Pfizer announced that its COVID-19 vaccine may be a remarkable 90% effective, based on early and incomplete test results that nevertheless brought a big burst of optimism to a world desperate for the means to finally bring the catastrophic outbreak under control.

The announcement came less than a week after an election seen as a referendum on President Donald Trump's handling of the virus. Trump had announced that the vaccine would arrive before the election and of course it landed 48 hours after Joe Biden was declared the winner of the election by the mainstream media—the same media both Fox News and CNN, MSNBC, to flat out censor any and all talk about voter fraud, claiming that Trump has no evidence.

President-elect Joe Biden has warned the United States is still 'facing a very dark winter' and says a COVID-19 vaccine likely won't be available for months despite the news today from Pfizer that its jab might be 90 percent effective.

Pfizer, which developed a vaccine with German drugmaker BioNTech, is the first to release successful data based on an interim analysis from a large-scale coronavirus vaccine clinical trial. Just hours after Pfizer's announcement, Biden made remarks from Wilmington, Delaware saying that a coronavirus vaccine approval process must be guided by science so the public can have confidence it is safe and effective.

Dr. Anthony Fauci, the U.S. government's top infectious-disease expert, said the results suggesting 90% effectiveness are "just extraordinary," adding: "Not very many people expected it would be as high as that."

President Trump had suggested repeatedly during the presidential campaign that a vaccine could be ready by Election Day and tweeted: "STOCK MARKET UP BIG, VACCINE

COMING SOON. REPORT 90% EFFECTIVE. SUCH GREAT NEWS!"

Pfizer has insisted that its work is not influenced by politics and that it was "moving at the speed of science." Denying that they were not part of the President's Operation Warp Speed program. Even though Pfizer denies it is playing politics, it is obvious that politics are at play here otherwise the vaccine would be distributed without delay, however, I am sure it will be held until the Electoral College votes in December and the transition of power happens between Biden and Trump.

So, will we have to wait until February for the vaccine to be available for the masses? This raises the question of whether using a virus as a weapon against a group of people is tantamount to terrorism.

The "Deep State's" mainstream media proxies launched a massive psy-op against the world by stoking fear about the virus, encouraging the continuous lockdowns, blaming the sitting President for the fatalities, and then by coincidence produce a vaccine with 90 percent effectiveness just three days after the announcement of a possible new president taking the White House.

It is also evident that the psy-op includes the declaring Biden the President-Elect despite the outcome still being litigated and the Electoral College not yet having cast their ballots for the Democratic candidate. Many average folks and foreign governments anticipate either innocent ignorance or willing hypocritical complicity with this take over due to their political sympathies for President Trump's opponents. In any case, just like "The Connection Between World War Covid & Psychological Processes Is Seriously Concerning," so too should the widespread manipulation of global perceptions be equally concerning for all those aware of what's happening.

Last month, an international group of lawyers claimed that they are preparing to sue the World Health Organization over the damage inflicted on large parts of the population by the coronavirus lockdowns.

A lawyer named Dr. Reiner Fuellmich is one of four members of the German Coronavirus Investigative Committee Claims. He, along with many lawyers, is taking evidence and listening to testimonies of large numbers of international scientists to 'find answers to questions that more and more people are asking worldwide about the Coronavirus'.

This corona crisis he says must be renamed a corona scandal and those responsible for it must be criminally prosecuted and sued for civil damages. He proceeds to explain how and where an international network of lawyers will argue this 'biggest tort case ever'. There are three main questions to answer: briefly, the first – is there a corona pandemic or a PCR testing pandemic? The second is lockdown (social distancing, masks, and so on) a protective measure, or is it there to create panic and fear? Third—were governments massively lobbied by the chief protagonists of the corona pandemic?

Meanwhile, Biden still contends that Dark Winter has arrived and that 200,000 more people will die if we do not wear masks and social distance—you may recall that he gave the same quote in August claiming if people would just wear their masks for three more months they would save nearly 200,000 lives. Now the lives he said would be saved are the same that will die if we don't comply.

If they're not freeing the vaccine and continue this psy-op this can be considered psychological terrorism.

Biden stated: "We are Americans, and our country is under threat."

COVID-19. Biden, Trump. Social Justice. War. Human Rights. Economics. Whatever the issue, it seems that every day we are being told we must adopt a particular position. And to do so "or else". Under incredible pressure to be in the right and to feel good about ourselves, we are bombarded with "ways to think" that is quite often delivered by overt propaganda, but that is also, perhaps more than we realize, covert and not aware to us consciously.

None of this is a coincidence, none of it is accidental, but it is sinister. If things continue as they have been, and this lockdown remains in place, whether fully or partially, the anticipation of this "dark winter" will be on the minds of almost all Americans, especially if it is continually used as the threat of things to come. With that in the minds of the people, they will be expecting the worst, and will probably get exactly what they expect; an extension of a lockdown or a restart happening sometime either during Thanksgiving or Christmas of 2020 where they will warn families not to gather at these times.

The cooler climate will keep COVID-19 spreading—we are hearing now that it is at its fever pitch and yet they are sitting on that vaccine. The other dear is that there are no guarantees about the harmful side effects of a vaccine that has been rushed to production.

There will be lockdowns—government pauses extended emergencies and tax collecting during the winter.

Contact tracing of individuals will become more and more evident at public gatherings and in the Shopping Malls this winter. Be advised that there are also plans for door-to-door visits from Health security officials during the harsh winter that will of course conduct welfare checks, provide food and services if needed and they may discourage family gatherings for the holidays.

The government announced that a contract for $138 million was been issued to fund the production of 500 million pre-filled COVID-19 vaccine "injection devices," this was before any vaccine was available or even in the test range. Does this sound like a well-planned political maneuver?

As any should be able to see, this is a complex, but an easily identifiable plot that is coming to fruition very quickly and with little resistance. It is planned down to the last detail, just as were all the practice runs that were acted out in the past.

COVID-19 is real and it's very deadly for at-risk members of the population, but the historically unprecedented full-spectrum paradigm-changing processes catalyzed by the world's uncoordinated attempt to contain it have been greatly influenced by psychological processes that continue to be taken advantage of in order to politically exploit the pandemic, the observation of which should be seriously concerning for everyone.

Every country of economic significance seems to be scrambling to prepare themselves for what their leaders appear to sincerely believe is the inevitable "Fourth Industrial Revolution", or "Great Reset," though they're going about it in different ways.

The expectation of a Marxist post-scarcity economy where the automation and digitalization of many jobs will lead to the large-scale replacement of many workers with AI is predicted to result in greater individual dependence on the government, which is preemptively being forced upon many of them through lockdowns and subsequent economic stimulus packages that might ultimately lead to a policy of so-called "universal basic income".

In order to enforce compliance, the authorities exaggerate the lethality of COVID-19 to keep the population imprisoned in the homes out of fear, while those who dare to venture outside are forced to wear masks even though their effectiveness in preventing infection isn't perfect like they've been officially portrayed. Masks also serve the purpose of psychologically reassuring the population that they can survive the pandemic. It is your protection from what is planned for Dark Winter.

Operation Dark Winter was the code name for a senior-level bio-terrorist attack simulation conducted on June 22–23, 2001. It was designed to carry out a mock version of a covert and widespread smallpox attack on the United States.

Clearly, Clyde Lewis and others are aware of what's coming, and they want us to be prepared for the "Dark Winter" or the Global Reset. This is supposed to be a currency reset is what happens when the global financial system maxes out. That can happen in many different ways, depending on what the current currency system looks like. Once we hit too much debt, the world's leaders turn to a currency reset to rejig the system.

2021 Looking into The Future

CHAPTER FOUR

EXTREME WEATHER WORLDWIDE

Each year the weather gets fiercer from climate change and what others refer to as global warming. Of course, no one agrees on the cause of our extreme weather. The winter of 2020 going into 2021 will be a harsh one with extreme Arctic Express weather dipping into the United States in the West, Midwest, and East Coast. Lots of snow in the forecast and bitter cold. The East Coast can expect some Nor'easters.

Most of us have been blessed and have never endured extreme hardships, war, extreme weather, starvation, incurable diseases, until now with the global pandemic. Today, we have access to instant news, weather, and we travel in our cars and zip through the skies in airplanes to near and far away places.

One thing I must reiterate in my books, humans have not been good Earthkeepers. We litter, we pollute, we buy useless material things that we seldom use and then toss. Our rivers, lakes, and oceans are polluted with plastics, needles, sewage, oil spills, and other toxic substances from pesticides. I have witnessed how coral reefs are dying from what is called, "bleaching. This is caused by global warming and warmer oceans, pollution from pesticides running from rivers into the oceans, and other toxins entering the ocean. Too much sunlight can also cause bleaching.

In the early 1970s, I traveled to Mexico with my parents in their pickup camper, and we watched raw sewage running from beaches into the ocean where people swim and catch fish.

Our lack of consideration for our planet has created many of the effects happening to our planet. Global warming is caused by increased concentrations of greenhouse gases in the atmosphere, mainly from human activities such as burning fossil fuels (CO^2), deforestation, and farming.

Air pollution has contributed to our crazy weather. Warming temperatures have caused a massive amount of methane release from the melting of the permafrost in the Arctic. Scientists agree that the Earth's rising temperatures are fueling longer and hotter summer temperatures, more frequent droughts, heavier rainfall, tornadoes, and more powerful hurricanes. But there's more to it than that, and the spraying of "chemtrails" by unmarked planes since the late 1990s may have contributed even more global warming.

There's speculation that Planet X aka Nibiru, our solar system's failed star, is exerting a greater gravitational pull on Earth than our sun.

The solar system appears to have a new ninth planet. Two planetary scientists, Konstantin Batygin and Mike Brown announced evidence that a body nearly the size of Neptune in 2016 during a press conference—but as yet unseen by the naked eyes. The ninth planet orbits the sun every 15,000 years. During the solar system's infancy 4.5 billion years ago, they say, the giant planet was knocked out of the planet-forming region near the sun. Slowed down by gas, the planet settled into a distant elliptical orbit, where it still lurks today. More will be included on Planet X in Chapter 3.

June through August 2020 produced record-breaking global heat. Siberia, one of the coldest places on Earth, experienced a record-breaking temperature of 100° degrees Fahrenheit. Temperatures in the small Siberian town of Verkhoyansk hit 100.4 degrees Fahrenheit in June, according to public-facing weather data. It's a record-high temperature in one of the fastest-warming places in the world. Siberia tends to experience large swings in temperature, but it's unusual for warmer-than-average temperatures to continue for so long—temperatures in Siberia have stayed well-above-average since 2019.

The Arctic Circle during the winter can drop to -90 degrees Fahrenheit. The average temperature for June in this region is 68 degrees Fahrenheit, so the new-record-high temperature was alarming. As of May 2020, Siberia's rivers broke up exceptionally early and it was already the hottest May on record in the area since records began in 1979. Due to the unusual heat, permafrost melting beneath tank supports resulted in a massive diesel spill in the region, which reached the Arctic Ocean.

Scientists are concerned about the dramatic swings in temperature in northwest Siberia in 2020 which are supposed to happen only once in 100,000 years, yet climate warming has changed all that, according to the climate scientist Martin Stendel. The Arctic is warming twice as fast as the rest of the planet through a process known as Arctic amplification. Another worrisome problem, according to the National Oceanic and Atmospheric Administration (NOAA), is Arctic ice melt has accelerated so much it is leading to seasonal snow cover that isn't as white and absorbs more sunlight, which leads to more warming and melting.

With those significant changes, it will affect the rest of the world. Melting ice in the Arctic leads to higher sea levels, and not just in the Arctic Ocean. Even the Antarctic in the Southern Hemisphere shows signs of increased melting. With less ice in the North and South poles, the world's oceans will warm, and this could cause the Earth's poles to shift, a theory that has not been proven.

The ice on the poles stabilize our planet, but what if there's massive ice melt? Would the planet shift its poles?

Recently a Russian TV crew flew over the Siberian tundra during the summer and spotted a massive crater 30 meters (100 feet) deep and 20 meters wide—huge in size, symmetry, and the explosive force of nature that it must have taken to have created it.

Scientists aren't certain how the huge hole, the ninth spotted in the region since 2013, formed. Some strange theories have been suggested in an area that supports oil and gas extraction from the Yamal Peninsula in northwest Siberia. Some theories claim a meteorite impact caused the holes, a UFO landing, or there was the collapse of a secret underground military storage facility or base.

Some scientists theorize the giant hole is linked to an explosive buildup of methane gas released from the permafrost. The same thing is taking place in Alaska and the Arctic region there.

"Right now, there is no single accepted theory on how these complex phenomena are formed," said Evgeny Chuvilin, lead research scientists at the Skolkovo Institute of Science and Technology's Center for Hydrocarbon Recovery, who has visited the site of the newest crater to study its features. "It is possible they have been forming for years, but it is hard to estimate the numbers. Since craters usually appear in uninhabited and largely pristine areas of the Arctic, there is often no one to see and report them," Chuvilin said.

CHAPTER FIVE

PLANET X THEORY

In the late 1940s, my mother, while attending the University of Moscow, Idaho, wrote a thesis on the Earth pole shift theory. From the research she was able to find at the time, she believed that Earth had shifted its poles many times, and at a future time, the Earth would shift again.

Interesting news recently shows that between South American and southern Africa, there is an enigmatic magnetic region called the South Atlantic Anomaly, where the magnetic field is a lot stranger than expected. Scientists believe that weak and unstable fields are thought to precede magnetic reversals and it might happen any time. A study, published on June 12, 2020, by the National Academy of Sciences, uncovered how long the field in the South Atlantic has been acting up. This might be a harbinger of a physical shift of the poles.

What scientists are sure of is that a weak magnetic field makes Earth more prone to magnetic storms that can knock out the electronic infrastructure, including the power grids.

The magnetic field of the South Atlantic Anomaly is already so weak that it has affected satellites and their technology when they fly past it. The strange region is believed to be related to a patch of magnetic field that is pointing a different direction to the rest at the top of the planet's liquid outer core at a depth of 1,795 miles (2,889 km) within the Earth.

Geologists at Rice University have uncovered evidence that suggests Earth's spin axis was in a different spot millions of years ago, a phenomenon called "true polar wander." The change happened around 12 million years ago and shifted Greenland further up into the Arctic Circle, which may have contributed to the onset of the last major Ice Age, 3.2 million years ago.

This axle has always stayed the same relative to the sun, giving our planet its characteristic axial tilt. But the North and South poles haven't always been the same. It shows at various times in our planet's history that the true poles have been in different places. New evidence of these shifts comes from an analysis of millions of years of data left behind in Earth's geological record—in the path of hotspots in Hawaii and sediments and magnetic fields taken from the seafloor.

Scientists found that between 48 million and about 12 million years ago, the Earth's spin axis, and therefore the geographic north and south poles, were in a different place than they are today. Long ago, the North Pole would have been closer to Greenland than it is now, and the South Pole would have shifted similarly to the west. Somewhere around 12 million years ago, the poles moved to where they are now.

Although geologists speculate that a massive asteroid hit the earth 65 million years ago and caused the extinction of the dinosaur, it might have caused an imbalance in the Earth's poles and caused them to change places.

Is there any evidence that the Sun once rose in the west and set in the east, the reverse of today? If the sun did rise in the west, this would certainly add more evidence of our planet flipping or a reverse of the Earth's rotation and hemispheres. If such a mega event occurred, our ancestors would have put down some form of ancient written or oral legend of this event.

Immanuel Velikovsky in his *World in Collision* book investigated ancient records that show evidence for a reversing of the sun rising and setting in ancient Egyptian records. Herodotus, the ancient Greek historian, wrote that four times during this period the sun rose contrary to his, twice it rose where it now set, and twice it set where it now rises.

Pomponius Mela, a Latin author of the first century wrote: "The Egyptians pride themselves on being the most ancient people in the world. In their authentic annals, one may read that since they have been in existence, the course of the stars has changed direction four times and that the sun has set twice in that part of the sky where it rises today."

The magical Papyrus Harris is the longest known papyrus from Egypt, with some 1,500 lines of text. It was found in a tomb near Medinet Habu, across the Nile River from Luxor, Egypt in 1855, and was sent to the British Museum in 1872. The ancient text speaks of a cosmic upheaval of fire and water when "the south becomes north, and the Earth turns over." In the Papyrus Ipuwer, it also tells of a great catastrophic event, and states that "the land turns around [over] as does a potter's wheel" and the "Earth turned upside down."

In the Egyptian tomb of Senmut, the architect of Queen Hatshepsut, a panel on the ceiling shows the celestial sphere with the signs of the zodiac and other constellations in "a reversed orientation" of the southern sky.

Caius Julius Solinus, a Latin author of the third century, wrote of the people living on the southern borders of Egypt, "The inhabitants of this country say that they have it from their ancestors the sun now sets where it formerly rose."

In the Syrian city of Ugarit (Ras Shamra) a poem was discovered dedicated to the planet-goddess Anat, who massacred the population of the Levant and who exchanged the two dawns and the position of the Stars.

The ancient Maya of Mexico wrote in hieroglyphics describing four movements of the sun, *'nahui ollin tonatiugh.'* These four motions refer to four prehistoric suns or world ages, with shifting cardinal points.

It's beyond coincidence that both the Egyptians and the ancient people of Mexico also referred to four events.

The Eskimos of Greenland related their legends to missionaries that in ancient times the Earth turned over and the people who lived then became antipodes. (the meaning of antipode is related to geography and any spot point on Earth's surface diametrically opposite to it).

Lastly, the Koran speaks of the Lord of two easts and two wests.

This shows that the people who run our world don't want us to know what is taking place on our planet and outside our planet.

On September 10, 1984, a news report from US News World questioned if Planet X was really out there. The report read that in 1983, the infrared astronomical satellite (IRAS), circling the polar orbit 560 miles from the Earth, detected heat from an object about 50 billion miles away that is now the subject of intense speculation. "All I can say is that we don't know what it is yet," said Gerry Neugebauer, director of the Palomar Observatory for the California Institute of Technology.

Then in 1992, NASA issued a press release, "Unexplained deviations in the orbits of Uranus and Neptune point to a large outer solar system body of 4 to 8 Earth masses on a highly tilted orbit, beyond 7billion miles from the Sun." A follow-up released stated, "Astronomers are so sure of the 10th planet, they think there is nothing left but to name it," stated Ray T. Reynolds, a researcher at NASA in a press release 1992.

Oddly, these stories were quickly retracted without any explanation.

December of 2015, I posted my predictions on my website and wrote this, *"Watch for NASA to announce more weird news on the planets and astonishing finds in our solar system and beyond. They are going to make some outrageous claims and maybe even an alien disclosure about ancient structures in outer space—Mars and the Moon."*

Then the most incredible news happened on January 20, 2016— two Caltech scientists, Brown and Batygin, gave a press conference and announced they had discovered the ninth planet in our solar system, 10 times the size of Earth. They believed it was Planet X. They calculated the massive body orbits the sun every 15,000 years.

Mike Brown and Konstantin Batygin, of the California Institute of Technology (Caltech) in Pasadena, California, were prepared for the inevitable skepticism with detailed analyses of its orbit and months of computer simulations. "If you say, 'We have evidence for Planet X,' almost any astronomer will say, 'This again? These guys are clearly crazy.' I would, too," Brown said. "Why is this different? This different because this time we're right."

If Planet X is out there, Brown and Batygin said that astronomers should find more objects in telltale orbits, shaped by the pull of the hidden giant. But Brown knows that no one will believe in the discovery until Planet X itself appears within a telescope viewfinder. "Until there's a direct detection, it's a hypothesis—even a potentially very good hypothesis," he said.

It's harder to explain why Planet X didn't either loop back around to where it started or leave the solar system entirely, but we know that most solar systems appear to have binary stars/suns, and Planet X might have been this solar system's second sun, that cooled and became a "Brown Dwarf" or failed star between 3 million and 10 million years ago. Now it's caught in an orbit through our solar system every 6,000 to 15,000 years.

Shortly after Brown and Batygin revealed the 9th planet, possibly Planet X, few articles were released on the subject.

Don't expect our leaders to admit to Planet X's journey through our solar systems and that it might be responsible for our extreme weather, increased seismic and volcanic activity. Already people are photographing a second huge object near the sun at dusk (check out YouTube videos).

Do I believe Planet X is out there and traveling through our Solar System? Absolutely! In the past few years, NASA has made comments on strange anomalies on the planet in our solar system without any explanation. If anything can cause our planet to shift its pole, it would be the strong magnetic pull from this supergiant.

Nancy Leider of ZetaTalk, who claims she was been told by Zeta extraterrestrials that Planet X will cause our planet to shift again as it has in the past. She further said the Earth would slow its rotation and stop for a few hours. One half of the Earth's hemisphere will be in total darkness (night) and the other half in sunlight. Within hours, the shift will take place and there will be hurricane-force winds, powerful earthquakes will shake the Earth for days, volcanoes will erupt and dormant volcanoes dormant will awaken. Coastal areas globally will be inundated by oceans. The safety areas in the United States will be the Southwest, areas of the Midwest, and places away from the West and East coasts. Look for areas with old geology.

Nancy has gotten geological and weather predictions right, but so far, the Zeta got it wrong about the shift happening in the 1990s.

Even the late prophet Edgar Cayce (1877-1945) who gave thousands of readings in a trance-like state foretold of an Earth shift in the year 2000. Thankfully, his prediction has yet to come true.

When will the shift take place? If my recurring dreams at the age of seven are correct, it will be in my lifetime—that could be soon. There will be signs in the Earth and the heavens for those who are awakened.

CHAPTER SIX

THE NEW CHILDREN

Question: I was so impressed with your predictions. You are so accurate. My question for your book is will there be a cure for autism? My adult son was diagnosed with autism and I am always looking for a cure. I pray for a miracle for him.

And from another concerned mother: Hello, I know you are focused on world events, but could you do some predictions about people with autism and developmental delays? I am a full-time caregiver to my 20-year-old son and it just seems like no one cares about people with disabilities. thank you.

Answer: Thank you for your excellent question on Autism. Autism affects an estimated 10 out of every 10,000 people, depending on the diagnostic criteria used. Most estimates that include people with similar disorders are two to three times greater. Autism strikes males about four times as often as females and has been found throughout the world in people of all racial and social backgrounds.

In all cases of autism, these beautiful souls decided to experience physical earthly challenges to advance spiritually. Often, the lessons and advancement apply to those who care for these individuals as well. Be assured that the caregivers of the world have great courage and are greatly honored for their care and compassion for these souls. They advance quickly as well.

A large number of autistic children are savants and demonstrate certain abilities far above average. A savant is a genius usually with one ability.

An example of this ability is Korean American, Kodi Lee, 23 years old, who won the 14th season of *America's Got Talent.* Kodi was born with optic nerve hypoplasia that rendered him legally blind at an early age. He is also autistic and suffered from Addison's Disease, which is a life-threatening disorder if not monitored.

Throughout his life, his mother was a positive force for him and noticed that he had a special talent in music at a very early age. He could play anything once he heard it. His goal in life is to share his music with the world and to make people happy.

This was why Kodi was reborn into this present life to share his beautiful spirit and the God-given gift he was given. Kodi has performed locally near his Lake Elsinore, California home at a variety of venues, including local restaurants, wineries, and performed in Las Vegas at the Paris Hotel. His musical repertoire ranges from rock and jazz to R&B and pop.

He is one of 25 people in the entire world that possesses such a keen ability for musical expression with perfect pitch and audio photographic memory, which means he can recall any music piece after hearing the song just once. He has mastered classics such as Bach, Chopin, Mozart, and others. He has learned how to tap dance and sing simultaneously.

Any child, no matter how physically, mentally, or emotionally challenged as Kodi is, can be incalculably helped and strengthened by the love and support of their parents. Kodi Lee is an extraordinary young man. Kodi chose to return at this time to show us pure love. Perhaps he is the embodiment of a Master. Remember Masters come in many sizes, shapes, and ethnic backgrounds to change our world.

Toxicity has probably contributed to autism. Seventy years ago, autism was rare. Our toxic environment, the additives in our food, meat, and pesticides on produce have contributed to autism, I believe. I also suspect that the aluminum and barium believed to be in the chemtrail spraying worldwide since the late 1990s has also caused increased autism. There are also theories about vaccines.

Another gifted developmentally challenged young man is Marshall Stewart Ball, 34-years old, who writes God-inspired poems. Marshall has a devastating genetic disorder that causes him to not be able to walk, talk, sit up without assistance, or to even feed himself. But his mind is lovely and free.

His book of poems, *Kiss of God,* was published in 1999. Marshall learned at age five how to communicate by pointing to specific letters on the alphabet board. There was never any doubt in Marshall's mind about his mission in life. Since the beginning of his writing life at age five, he has been a "teacher."

He said this, *I see myself as a teacher that knows about God. Good thoughts come to me and they teach.*

Marshall wants all of us to learn to be better listeners, better thinkers, and simply better people. For many years he told his mother that he "listens." At times, she watched him quietly looking off into the distance, eyes slightly raised as if he truly seemed to be listening.

At the age of seven-years-old he wrote these words, *To judge another is to judge God.* At the age of eight, he wrote, *Destruction is the need to find being in matter.* And this: *Marshall has been here for millions of lifetimes.* Marshall came into this world knowing he had been here millions of times through reincarnation.

Marshall wrote this during his youth. *Twenty years in the future we see a world that has a time of perfect harmony. Perhaps man will become loving. Answers need to come about how people see God. Realize a good God will bring harmony.*

Marshall can be contacted at marshall@marshallball.com. Please allow him plenty of time to respond.

It's a shame that most of us have a preconceived idea of what a Spiritual Master should look like, but they are here and in bodies, we don't expect. If we could learn to be of pure heart and soul like Marshall, our world would be a more spiritual place.

Edgar Cayce (1877-1945) gave thousands of readings in a trance-like state on medical cures and diagnosed people throughout the world. He said autism in some cases is caused by pressures along the spine where the nerve plexus coordinates the functioning of the system. Nervous system incoordination resulted in producing a disturbance to the "imaginative nerve forces of the body" causing the child to be "oversensitive." Conceptually, the Cayce approach to autism focuses on assisting the body in healing itself by the application of a variety of therapies intended to address the underlying causes of the condition. The mental and spiritual aspects of healing are strongly emphasized.

Here are some general therapeutic recommendations intended to address the underlying causes of autism:

1. MANUAL THERAPY (SPINAL MANIPULATION): Cayce often recommended spinal manipulations to correct specific problems which may be a primary cause of autism. It is difficult to obtain the osteopathic adjustments specified by Cayce. However, a chiropractor may be of help. The frequency of the adjustments will depend on the recommendations of the individual chiropractor or osteopath. The use of an electric vibrator may also be helpful for individuals unable to obtain regular spinal adjustments.

2. ELECTROTHERAPY: Regular use of the Radial Appliance to coordinate nerve functioning and circulation is recommended.

3. INTERNAL CLEANSING: Because autistic symptoms were sometimes linked to problems with the alimentary canal resulting in poor eliminations, hydrotherapy is recommended to improve eliminations through the colon. Hydrotherapy includes drinking six to eight glasses of pure water daily and obtaining colonic irrigations to cleanse the bowel. Following the diet should also assist with internal cleansing. Hot castor oil packs applied over the abdomen are recommended to improve circulation (especially lymphatic) and eliminations through the alimentary canal.

4. DIET: The Basic Cayce Diet is intended to improve assimilation and elimination. The diet focuses heavily on keeping a proper alkaline/acid balance while avoiding foods that produce toxicity and drain the system. Essentially, the diet consists mainly of fruits and vegetables while avoiding fried foods and refined carbohydrates ("junk food"). Certain food combinations are emphasized.

5. SUGGESTIVE THERAPEUTICS: The use of positive suggestions during the pre-sleep period and during therapy sessions (such as massage and the Radial Appliance) is

recommended to awaken the inner healing response. The spiritual attunement of the caregiver is essential.

6. MEDICATION: The use of a mild natural sedative (such as Passionflower fusion) may be helpful for excitable children.

In the 1970s, the Indigo children or Generation X began coming into the planet. Now, adults, they were gifted children, on a clear mission to challenge and shift reality. Beyond psychic awareness, they are highly driven and creative with a perception that sees through the established norms of society. Old souls indeed, their mission is clearly laid out to shake up the modern world and pave the way for future generations to create greater peace and harmony for all.

The Millennials are far different from any generation and they have been dubbed the "me generation. They began incarnating here a little over twenty years ago. There are plenty of articles and videos on them that they are narcissistic and self-centered, and in some cases they are. I know from personal experience. Because they are so connected to their cell phones and computers, they are influenced by what they see and hear on social media. In other words, they are the lemmings of our generation. Many of the Millennials are now the ones protesting, angry about politics, about police, about bigotry, about abuse, and the only way they see fit to get their message across is with anger and violence.

Of course, not all people feel that way and have been in peaceful protests in large cities. Those who believe violence is the only way to bring about change have a hard lesson to learn that it can never be achieved in negative ways.

Large numbers of young people seem to demonstrate a lack of compassion for the misfortunes of others. In fact, some mock those with health problems and disabilities. What they don't realize that what they do to others, what they think, and what say, will come back to them either in this life or the next. It is called Karma, the Law of Cause and Effect. It's the Cosmic Boomerang!

Studies have found that Millennials believe in God, but they don't practice any religion or spirituality. Some explore the dark side and are involved in occult practices which is extremely dangerous. Perhaps it is because they don't believe in anything—a form of nihilism. They have been conditioned by violent video games and movies that numb them to their surroundings and world events. Even more frightening is antidepressant medications and opioids prescribed freely by doctors in the United States and other countries. One in eight Americans over the age of 12 have taken an antidepressant drug. That's alarming! That means most Americans are numb and emotionless to their surroundings if they remain on antidepressants. Some studies show that these drugs can help severely depressed people, but there are side effects of long-term use. I have seen friends turn into emotionless zombies. They are blocking their intuitive sixth sense and their natural emotions to function in day to day life. The one thing that makes humans, human—our emotions!

A great many young people are spiritual and are drug and alcohol-free. They are special souls in the world who know they have a mission to help humanity and they are making incredible changes with their inventions and creativity to help save our environment. They are the silent Masters, born at this time in history to make positive, peaceful changes for our planet.

For those seeking a well-respected medical intuitive, I suggest Kir Noel (www.healingabody.com), who is amazing. Clients have gone to her and highly recommend her.

In the year 2027, I do foresee children, not adults, coming down with some type of flu that will make take many lives. Remember that events are not set in stone and that humans through their consciousness are constantly changing timelines.

CHAPTER SEVEN

SMOKE AND MIRRORS

Josh Good lived in an apartment near the Trade Towers. He captured what happened that day and knows the 2nd Trade Building was not hit by a plane as we were told. I have always known that our government was involved with this horrendous act that killed 2,977 people that day. Josh wrote this on Youtube: This is the video I recorded on 9/11/2001 from the roof of my apartment on the corner of Fulton Street and William Street, and then continues on the street going towards the WTC on Fulton Street. The video begins as I ran onto the roof of my apartment building and continues until right before the 1st building came down. I was standing 1 block away. The footage is hard to see with the people leaping to their death stories above the ground. I am surprised the video has not been removed by YouTube.

https://www.youtube.com/watch?v=siYkDNbeRZk

September 11, 2001 was a prime event that changed the course of human history. There are stories of those who worked at the Trade Tower building that were given warnings not to go into work or were miraculously delayed from getting to work and saved. Did some foresee this event? Hundreds did have a foreboding of something happening.

I dreamed one year before the event of a huge apple tree. The dream was like watching a movie where this huge tree had apples and was beautiful and green. Suddenly the leaves began to wither, and the apples drop. Then the entire tree was sucked into the ground and vanished. The dream was a symbol but at the time I didn't understand the symbology until after 9-11. The apple tree in my dream represented New York City, nicknamed "The Big Apple" in the 1920s.

My premonition was showing me that by the way it was pulled straight down into the ground that the World Trade Buildings were downed not by planes, but by an implosion by explosives. There's so much more I could add to what happened on that day, but most people would not believe my visions of the events that lead to the attack and the well-known people involved.

As more time goes by and the younger generation becomes adults and the real events of on that day will be a distant memory of planes going into the two tallest buildings in New York City on September 11, 2001, killing nearly 3,000 people. History has and will continue to be manipulated and changed to what historians want us to believe. It's happened in the far past, and it's happening now. Lately, any conspiracy theories video that once abounded on YouTube is hard to find or on Google and other search engines. Most are debunked and skeptics.

The Trade Towers were constructed in the 1970s and were built to withstand a plane crashing into them with the strongest steel and reinforcement, yet on 9-11-2001, the two-building fell within minutes of being hit by commercial planes and pancaked down as if explosives were set inside them. It appeared to be a demolition explosion. Experts have given pro and con theories on their destruction, and no one seems to agree whether explosive could have been used, but firefighters and police and other first responders heard and witnessed what appeared to be explosions in the buildings.

But here is the strangest part of this prime event. Proponents of the World Trade building demolition theories allege that the number 7 building —a 47-story skyscraper that stood across Vesey Street north of the main part of the World Trade Center site, was intentionally destroyed with explosives. Unlike the Twin Towers, which appeared to be giant 11s reaching into the sky, number 7 World Trade Center was not hit by a plane, although it was damaged by fires that burned for seven hours until it collapsed.

Unlike the Twin Towers, 7 World Trade Center was not hit by a plane, although it was hit by debris from the Twin Towers and was damaged by fires which burned for seven hours, until it collapsed completely at about 5:20 p.m. on the evening of September 11. It was a new building and opened in May of 2006. Several videos of the collapse event exist in the public domain, thus enabling comparative analysis from different angles of perspective.

Isn't it interesting that the 9/11 Commission Report and the Federal body charged with investigating the event, required seven years to conduct its investigation and issue a report? Time to cover up the facts. Conspiracy theorists maintain that building 7 was demolished because it may have served as an operational center for the demolition of the Twin Towers, while others suggest that government insiders may have wanted to destroy key files held in the building about corporate fraud.

The WTC buildings housed dozens of federal, state, and local government agencies. What was so important to destroy and kill 3,000 people in the process?

2021 Looking into The Future

CHAPTER EIGHT

THE CLONES

As absurd as this story may sound, our world is being manipulated not only by the Family of Dark (humans) but by extraterrestrials and possibly genetically cloned humans invading our cities with an unknown agenda.

Dr. Ardy Sixkiller Clark, a former Professor at Montana State University, spent years traveling and interviewing indigenous people from the Southwest to Central America about their encounters with extraterrestrials for her book, *Encounters with Star People.* I had the opportunity to interview her twice on my Rainbow Vision Talk Show in 2015, and I found her to be truthful and articulate about the indigenous people she spoke to who allowed her to interview them because of her Native American roots. The name Sixkiller is Dr. Clark's Cherokee surname.

Dr. Clark said she first learned about the "Star People, from her grandmother who told her ancient legends of her people.

She talked to Willie Joe, a university-educated Navajo in his mid-forties at the time. She met Willie in the late spring of 1987 and had just attended a conference in Phoenix. While driving through the Navajo Reservation, she stopped to look at the roadside jewelry stands. At one booth, she spotted an alien head keychain fashioned from silver with inlaid turquoise eyes. She discovered the owner of the stand had an artist cousin who made the keychain. While talking to the owner of the stand, she asked if he believed in Star People, and he said that UFOs visited the reservation often. He admitted to seeing spacecraft on several occasions, but he had never seen an extraterrestrial. After she explained her interest, the stand owner went to his car and dialed his mobile phone and began to speak in his native Navajo tongue. When he returned, he said Willie Joe would meet with her at the Holiday Inn restaurant in Chinle for breakfast the next day. He described his cousin to Clarke as wearing a big black cowboy.

Clarke met Willie Joe at 7:00 a.m. and had only two hours to talk before he had to get work. Willie Joe was a short, stout, muscular man with laughing eyes and an infectious smile. She began the conversation about his cousin and how he had mentioned his experiences with Star People and UFOs.

Clarke switched on her tape recorder and Willie Joe began, "My life has never been my own. From the time I was born, I had a twin, not in the sense of a biological twin, but a twin created by aliens from my blood and nurtured by them on some far distant planet. Every year they came and took me to him. We would play together for a while, and then they would take us into a room, connect us up to machines, and check us out. I always thought they were transferring my knowledge to him. I grew up always knowing they could come at any time. I don't know why they needed a duplicate of me. Maybe they considered us disposable people."

Clarke then asked, "Is that what you believe? Do you think the aliens are making a double so they can replace you here on Earth?"

Willie stopped and smoothed back his black hair and looked out the window. "When I was a kid, I believed they were capable of just about anything. I was not the only child taken and duplicated. When they would come and take me to their spaceship, I saw others just like me. Over time, there were hundreds, maybe thousands of us taken, from all races. For some reason, I always believed our government knew about it. Maybe they considered us disposable people." He poured cream into his coffee with three packets of sugar and continued. Clarke then asked, "Was there any particular reason that made you believe the government was cooperating with the aliens?"

Perhaps I was just paranoid. After all, I'm Indian and distrust of the government is part of our DNA," he laughed. "Or, maybe, it's something I learned during my abductions. Now that I am older and hopefully wiser, I think I was no more than an experiment, but for some reason, I still believe the government knows about it."

"Why do you think the government would cooperate?" Clarke asked.

"Simple. If the aliens are superior and stronger than humans and our government, it would be only natural for them to cooperate, perhaps out of fear or maybe to gain favors from the aliens."

"Favors?"

Willie Joe answered, "Maybe advanced technology. I think that's the reason the government is so vehement in their denials of the existence of aliens. How could you ever admit to the American people that you are allowing aliens to experiment on humans in return for technological advancement? So, what you do is throw up a smokescreen, find a few academics to write books, and make the people who come forth look like idiots. Humiliate them and poke fun at them. That way they keep the truth submerged."

Clarke then asked if he thought his "double" had his personality.

He replied with a smile, "There were somethings I kept to myself. For example, if they did put him (his replica) in my place on Earth, I don't think he would understand our culture. He would be an outsider. It would be like a white man reading about Diné (a Navajo word for Navajo people) ways, but not having them as part of his soul. These aliens can intercept a man's body. They can copy his body, but they can't take his soul. I think they're without a soul. So, they may get an identical body in shape, form, voice, but the soul or the spirit can't be duplicated. This duplicate could never be a real Diné."

For several years, Clarke kept in touch with Willie Joe. His story never changed throughout the years. He was proud that he never drank and prided himself on being a role model for the young people in his community. During her last visit, Willie Joe confided in Clarke that he was diagnosed with pancreatic cancer, and he thought his sickness, his cancer, was related to his abduction. He said the aliens stopped abducting him a few months earlier. He believed they knew he had cancer. "They are not so omnipotent. If they were, they could cure this cancer. Or maybe again, they were finished with me."

During their last dinner visit, Clarke asked Willie Joe how he felt about his captors. She asked what he felt was the greatest impact for him regarding the abductions.

He spoke after several minutes, "When I was young, I wanted to marry and have lots of kids. I was from a large family and Navajos love big families. I never married because I was always afraid that they would take one of my children and make a reproduction. I did not want to condemn a child to that fate."

"But you said they never hurt you," she commented.

"That's true. But they stole my privacy, my right to live my life without interference. All a man needs in this world is the respect of his friends and relatives. He needs to live his life with dignity. They never treated me with dignity. I only ask one thing of them. I want to know what gave them the right to kidnap human children, but they never told me."

These were Willie Joe's final words before he and Clarke departed never to see each other again. "I have been thinking lately about dying. I have only a few months left, but if you do write your book, I want you to make sure you tell my story. People need to know that these abductions are much more than curiosity or medical exams. There is a malevolence about them. Parents need to know that, if children tell stories about a twin, or strangers who come into their bedroom at night, listen to them. Chances are they are like me."

Clarke assured him that she would tell his story.

"Perhaps that's the reason I am here on this Earth, to meet you and tell you my story. That way, when you write your book, my story will be told, and I will have fulfilled the purpose of my life. I do believe each of us has a purpose."

Willie Joe passed away five months later without leaving any descendants.

Most of us have heard from friends or family that they have seen someone exactly like them—a cloned lookalike. Both my mother and I were told by friends that they had seen us in different parts of the country, but these are places we've never visited. I suspect that we all have alien twins—perhaps millions of duplicates exist. This is a frightening prospect for our future.

Let's hope that what Willie Joe witnessed with the clone-like beings unloaded from spaceships and driving to our cities, mixing with humans, isn't for some dark plan. What if some of the rioters aren't human, but clones of humans? Were the clones programmed to incite riots and mayhem in our cities? Nothing surprises me anymore with technology.

Clarke included another bizarre story involving clone humans, which begs the questions if true—why are aliens creating clones that resemble living humans? Several sources claim that human-looking alien beings have intergraded into human society and currently live in major cities. Further study on us seems out of the question because they have been experimenting on us for eons. If they planned a takeover of the Earth, it would seem more feasible they'd have done it before we developed nuclear weapons. Or could they the ones responsible for the chaos and escalating tensions throughout the world?

Clarke had met two other Native Americans who claimed to have either encountered a twin clone or seen aliens dropping off cloned humans on their reservation. Our government knows what is going on and the alien's ultimate agenda, yet they allow it, probably because they want greater technology in exchange for the aliens experimenting on us. Are they biological robots here to monitor humans? Is there a planned invasion about to take place? With everything going on in the world, I suspect that thousands and maybe even millions of clone-like humans are among us, and they are here to create massive chaos.

Question: You have written about UFO and aliens and experienced your own UFO sightings and possible alien encounter. Do you believe that benevolent beings are here to help us as well as the dark, malevolent beings that experiment on humans and work with the U.S. military?

Answer: There are so many clandestine projects going on in our world now, and most are not for the good of mankind. However, I believe benevolent beings are assisting us, including angelic beings and they are stepping in to stop the dark forces gathering around us. Already we are seeing what is happening in our country with the satanic practices, but this is just the surface of what is happening in secret by the Elite. When we run from the dark, we give it more power, allowing it to grow. We have denied this force for far too long—eons in our history. A spiritual war is taking place on Earth.

The Racists and Terrorists

Question: BLM and Antifa are groups that advocate violence and bigotry. What do you foresee happening with these groups?

Answer: BLM (Black Lives Matters) are an extension of souls who reincarnated from another time where they were killed for their beliefs. They returned at this time period with hate and anger lingering in their consciousness, vowing to do achieve their rights through violence. They have not learned that violence doesn't work.

These young people have not spiritually advanced. In some instances, they have a right to be angry about the deaths of black people by jittery police. Some police and law enforcement are prejudice, and some haven't been trained properly, but we greatly need them in this violent world.

The violence that erupted after George Floyd died by a chokehold was not justified and neither was the BLM protests that to shootings, looting, and burning in major cities. Sadly, a large percentage of the businesses that burned in cities were owned by black people.

Here's a flashback: A similar event happened in Watts, California from August 11, 1965, to August 16, 1965, known as the "Watts Riots." It began when a black woman was stopped in her car for reckless driving. A minor argument broke out and then escalated into a fight with the police. Community members spread a rumor that the woman was pregnant, and six days later civil unrest followed. Thirty-four people died and over $40 million in property damage to the African American community. It was the worst unrest since the death of Rodney King in 1992.

I understand the resentment that has been brewing for the past centuries from inequality, slavery, and bigotry over the color of one's skin. But violence doesn't solve anything, it only grows until there's an explosive situation. Racial and religious bigotry has always existed in our history. Until we learn to accept all races, a person's sexual orientation, and religious beliefs our world will continue to have bloody wars and violence due to our inability to love one another. Black lives do matter but so does all Life on Earth.

Clyde Lewis said it best on his Ground Zero talk show recently, "We are learning the hard way that everything is connected to everything. Freedom—we can no longer say we are a land that is united in the concept of freedom. We are all participating in a ritual that destroys our dignity and humanity."

Without the Family of Dark outrageously, preposterously trashing every single one of our values and boundaries, we will never awaken. We would continue to be complacent, never noticing what was transpiring under our noses. The outrage, the shock, the distress of trust, will increase to a frequency never seen before. You can't imagine the control agenda in store for us. When we examine the ancient civilizations that met with similar divisions, secrets societies, and hidden power, we discover that anything hidden from our view, kept from us, is corrupt. The elites who control our world and think they control us, are puppets themselves.

Antifa

Antifa is regarded as a militant, left-wing, anti-fascist political activist movement in the US, comprises autonomous activist groups that aim to achieve their political objectives through the use of direct action rather than through policy reforms. Groups like this don't want peace and harmony. Again, I reiterate, that these people are puppets and are mere tools to carry out more chaos and destruction. We could become another Nazi Germany if we don't awaken to what is taking place. It's up to us not to let this happen, ever!

You feel so lost, so cut off, so alone, only you're not. See,

in all our searching, the only thing we've found that makes the
emptiness bearable, is each other. —
1997 movie, CONTACT

CHAPTER NINE

THE FUTURE OF FREQUENCIES

2020 became the year of "I CAN'T BREATHE" and the Universe heard our words and granted it. Those words were chanted over and over by BLM protest (Black Lives Matter) after the death of George Floyd and that created resonance. Next, people worldwide became infected with the Coronavirus and were gasping for air—they could not breathe as their lungs filled with fluid, and then the summer of 2020 came one of the worst years for horrific wildfires throughout the Western United States set by lightning and mostly arsonists. Thick smoke blanketed northern and southern California, Oregon, Washington, Arizona, and Idaho. Again, people found they could not breathe. Smoke from the wildfires traveled 2,500 miles to the East Coast during the 2020 summer months.

Those words and thoughts created a resonance through our negative chanting. Instead, we should be chanting, "It's a blessing to breathe" instead of "I can't breathe." Our words have consequences.

If you doubt that words and thoughts are that powerful and can create our reality consider this: NOAA's GOES 8 and GOES 10 satellites showed on 9-11-2001 shortly after the first plane hit the Trade Tower that a huge spike occurred in the Earth's geomagnetic field. GOES 8, while orbiting 22,300 miles around the equator that day detected the first surge that topped out at nearly 50 units or Nano Teslas, higher than any reading previously recorded. The time was 9 am Eastern Standard Time, 15 minutes before the second plane supposedly hit the other build. We are connected as magnetic beings and to the Earth—the plants, the trees, the insects, the animals, the water, the rocks, and the entire universe. Yet we feel so alone, so isolated.

We need to remember that everything has consciousness and we do affect our physical world with our powerful words and thoughts.

Greek philosopher Pythagoras, born 600 B.C. in Phoenicia, understood resonance and envisioned the universe as a harmonious whole and believed that everything emitted a sound or a "vibration." He viewed the Earth and the planets as globes orbiting around a central luminary—the sun. Following his discovery that strings of different lengths produced different notes when plucked, he theorized that each planet had a note of its own, which depended upon its distance from the center. When combined these planetary sounds should produce a "harmonious cosmic octave."

Numbers (resonance) are called the physical constants of the universe, and without them, you would not exist. These mysterious numbers describe things like the speed of light or the strength of the electromagnetic force that holds atoms and molecules together.

In the Old Testament Book of Genesis, it states how the Universe was created by the "Word of God" which was a vibration, a sound that had enormous force and creation.

Today, we know it is a scientific fact that certain frequencies can kill and destroy physical matter; even a soprano's high note can shatter glass. Even the ancient people believed that it was possible to discover and apply the "Word of God" for their own needs. Special words and music were used for invocations and the success achieved was thought to depend on the vibration and the pitch of the sound chosen because music as well as words can be related to numbers. Low vibrations are destructive and higher vibrations are healing.

A good example of low vibration happened to the Tacoma Narrows Bridge, a suspension bridge in the State of Washington that spanned the Tacoma Narrows strait of Puget Sound between Tacoma and the Kitsap Peninsula, that collapsed. At the time of its construction and destruction, the bridge was the third-longest suspension bridge in the world in terms of main span length, behind the Golden Gate Bridge in San Francisco and the George Washington Bridge. From the time the deck was built on July 1, 1940, it began to move vertically in windy conditions. The motion was detected during the time it was opened to the public, and several measures were tried to stop the movement.

The bridge's collapse under 40 mph winds on November 7, 1940. The bridge's collapse changed science and engineering in many ways—in physics textbooks, the event is presented as an example of elementary forced resonance, with the wind providing an external periodic frequency that matched the bridge's natural structural frequency. Many believed the bridge's failure was due to aeroelastic flutter. Today, the study of bridge aerodynamics-aeroelastics has influenced the designs of all the world's great long-span bridges built since 1940.

Resonance is also believed to have brought down the walls of Jericho during the Battle of Jericho. According to the Book of Joshua, the Battle of Jericho was the first battle of the Israelites in their conquest of Canaan. In Joshua 6:1-27, the walls of Jericho fell after Joshua's Israelite army marched around the city blowing their trumpets seven times.

Did mechanical resonance from marching around the City of Jericho and the trumpets cause the fabled walls to collapse? Scientists say it's probable. Acoustical resonance can collapse bridges and buildings as demonstrated by earthquakes and winds. Some Bible scholars believe that Joshua used the Arch of the Covenant to bring down the walls of Jericho.

There are also stories of humans swaying to the music on 2nd-floor buildings causing the floor to collapse.

In the year 2000, London's Millennium Bridge was shut down after a crowd created oscillating waves across the deck of the bridge.

In 2016, American government employees in Cuba came down with mystifying symptoms—dizziness, insomnia, difficulty concentrating, after hearing a strange high-pitched sound. All the employees had one thing in common—damage to the part of the inner ear responsible for balance.

Doctors at the University of Miami confirmed in a scientific paper that the U.S. government employees had a real condition and not the result of mass hysteria. To the 26 people affected, the events felt like something out of "Star Trek." A few minutes of high-pitched noise, often accompanied by a high-pressure sensation, described as a "force field," was felt in their homes and hotel rooms in Cuba over several months and changed their lives, and in some cases, ended careers due to horrendous side effects.

More than a year after the episodes began, the Trump administration sent most of the embassy personnel home, leaving 18 people in Havana. Now, 26 people based in Havana have been identified with "otherwise-unexplained, medically-confirmed symptoms and clinical finds" since late 2016, the State Department said in a statement.

The people affected have shown symptoms similar to those noted following a concussion or minor traumatic brain injury, including dizziness, headaches, hearing loss, and balance, visual and cognitive problems. The State Department officials categorized the events in Havana as attacks. Canada also reported similar cases affecting several of its diplomats in Cuba.

The prominent theory is a type of microwave-based weapon was used on U.S. government employees. I sense that someone was testing a low-frequency modulation weapon in Cuba. These powerful weapons will be used to stun or kill people during riots, protests, and during wars. Such weapon will bring down buildings and structures.

A Star Trek future is upon us and some of the technology will be wonderful and other inventions disturbing.

CHAPTER TEN

THE ENERGY GRID

Question: I was reading your post today regarding a possible "systems crash" and would be grateful if you would comment more on this in your book. Do you see this frying electronics or a temporary system down, like the internet? I check your posts daily and love your work.

Answer: The sun has suddenly become very active in October. I expect sometime between now and 2021 that an X-Class flare will be aimed at Earth and cause a massive blackout and problems for the ISS (International Space Station). Hackers have also become extremely advanced in getting into corporations, financial institutions, and government records. Already there are those terrorists who want to bring down America any way they can and knowing how we are all dependent on the internet highway, a blackout or grid shutdown would be devastating even for one week.

On Sunday, Nov. 8th, giant sunspots AR2781 produced a <u>C5-class</u> solar flare, shown here in a photo from NASA's Solar Dynamics Observatory: the pulse of X-rays and UV radiation ionized the top of Earth's atmosphere, causing a brief shortwave radio blackout over Australia and the Indian Ocean (see the map below). Mariners, aviators, and ham radio operators in the region may have noticed unusual propagation at frequencies below 10 MHz. The entire episode lasted less than 20 minutes.

Stronger eruptions are possible. Sunspot AR2781 has a "beta-gamma" magnetic field that harbors energy for <u>M-class</u> flares, 10 times more intense than a C-flare. NOAA forecasters say there is a 15% chance of such an eruption on Nov. 8th.

We forget that our sun can produce massive coronal mass ejections. On the morning of September 1, 1859, amateur astronomer Richard Carrington ascended into the private observatory attached to his country estate outside of London. After cranking open the dome's shutter to reveal the clear blue sky, he pointed his brass telescope toward the sun and began to sketch a cluster of enormous dark spots that freckled its surface. Suddenly, Carrington spotted what he described as "two patches of intensely bright and white light" erupting from the sunspots. Five minutes later the fireballs vanished, but within hours their impact would be felt across the globe.

That night, telegraph communications around the world failed and there were reports of sparks showering from telegraph machines, shocking operators, and setting papers ablaze. All over the planet, colorful auroras illuminated the nighttime skies, glowing so brightly that birds began to chirp, and laborers started their daily chores, believing the sun had begun rising. Some thought the end of the world was at hand, but Carrington's naked eyes had spotted the true cause for the bizarre happenings: a massive solar flare with the energy of 10 billion atomic bombs. The flare spewed electrified gas and subatomic particles toward Earth, and the resulting geomagnetic storm—dubbed the "Carrington Event"—was the largest on record to have struck the planet.

Telegraph lines across North America were inoperable on August 28 as the first of two successive solar storms struck. A telegraph manager in Pittsburgh, reported that the resulting currents flowing through the wires were so powerful that platinum contacts were in danger of melting and "streams of fire" were pouring forth from the circuits.

On the morning of September 2, the magnetic mayhem continued for telegraph operators with the second storm. The atmosphere was so charged that operators made an incredible discovery—they could unplug their batteries and still transmit the message to Portland, Maine, at 30 to 90-second intervals using only the auroral current. By 10 am the magnetic disturbance abated enough that stations reconnected their batteries, but transmissions were still affected for the rest of the morning. Another effect was sky turned crimson causing people to believe there were huge fires in the cities.

Ice core samples have determined that the Carrington Event was twice as big as any other solar storm in the last 500 years. According to a 2008 report from the National Academy of Sciences, if such an event happened today, it would cause "extensive social and economic disruptions" due to the impact on power grids, satellite communications, the ISS (International Space Station), and GPS systems failing. The potential outages and damage would cost us today $1 trillion to $2 trillion.

I foresee either an energy grid or the internet going down by a solar event or terrorist attack.

2021 Looking into The Future

CHAPTER ELEVEN

THE TRUTH ABOUT CHEMTRAILS

Something transformational is taking place on Earth, our unique blue planet tucked away on the outer edge of the Milky Way Galaxy. Extreme weather, record-breaking heat in the summer of 2020, unimaginable wildfires that have destroyed hundreds of homes, and some lives in California, Oregon, Washington, and Idaho. At the beginning of the year, I had a vision of wildfires raging through thousands of acres, consuming everything in their path, and how drought conditions made it easy for arsonists to start the fires. However, not all the fires were started by arsonists. Some started from lightning or careless campers.

What caused the pines trees and all the brush to become so flammable in the past twenty years? What caused the pine trees to be unable to fight against the beetle invasions when they had survived the insects for centuries?

I, among other conspiracy theorists, believe the chemtrails that began in the late 1990s have contributed to global warming as well as fossil fuels and caused a massive die-off of trees and other plants.

Strange still was the way Coronavirus swept across the globe in record time and killed nearly one million souls at the time. I was shown the horrible flu late in 2019 that would be like the Spanish Flu, but at the time I couldn't conceive of such a horrible pandemic because of our advanced medical technology since the flu of 1917. Little did I foresee how it would affect our lives so drastically, and how thousands of be infected throughout the world. Coronavirus was different from any flu humans had ever had due to China's biological experiments and carelessness.

Unfortunately, humans haven't learned that technology in the wrong hands can be our ultimate extinction.

You see, I grew up when my generation, the Baby Boomers, believed that we would see the Age of Aquarius where love and peace abounded in our world. But it was only a dream and not reality.

Earth is experiencing increased seismic and volcanic activity while our Sun stays strangely quiet—few sunspots. Birds are dropping dead in the sky; sea creatures are dying and insects all over the world.

During this year, I have received countless email questions that I couldn't answer each personally. I will include those questions in this book and answer them from what I have seen in visions and sense intuitively will happen in 2021. If we thought 2020, was crazy, you haven't seen anything yet. 2021 will bring about massive changes to humanity in so many ways both positive and negative—but it will be a tumultuous year in politics, earth changes, weather anomalies, UFOs, medicine, travel, and saber-rattling countries.

Beginning in the late 1990s, I photographed and studied the chemtrail phenomenon and noted how the chemtrails always became heavy with crisscrossed patterns in the sky before an approaching weather front. Rain was usually forecast and then suddenly the clouds formed but there was no precipitation. It was odd. Then others began investigating the chemtrails spread by white, unmarked jets, and the conspiracy spread worldwide that a huge covert operation was in place.

In the past five years, we have witnessed unimaginable wildfires in the western United States and the rain forests of Brazil.

Author Denis Mills discovered an alarming link between chemtrails and the super wildfires while researching his novel, *Matt Legend—Veil of Lies*. He discovered that unprecedented levels of aluminum and barium nano-dust, primary components in chemtrails, both of which are incendiary, are fueling the ferocity of the super wildfires.

A retired USAF brigadier general, Gen. Charles Jones, has been quoted from a public source as stating, "These white aircraft spray trails are the result of scientifically verifiable spraying of aluminum particles and other toxic heavy metals, polymers and chemicals. Millions of tons of aluminum and barium are being sprayed almost daily across the U.S., stated Mills, a former naval officer, and UCLA graduate. "Just sprinkle aluminum or barium dust on fire and see what happens. It's near explosive. When wildfires break out, the aluminum/barium dust results in levels of fire intensity so great as to cause firefighters to coin a new term—'firenadoes,' " he said.

The government has denied the existence of chemtrail spraying for years. However, it is now called by various names under geoengineering.

According to Cal Fire Operation Chief Steve Crawford, the fires are burning differently and more aggressively. It has been reported the fires move faster than anyone has ever seen before and the barriers that in years past contained them, such as rivers, no longer work.

Another interesting fact—in Northern California's Mt. Shasta region, Francis Mangel, a USDA biologist took samples of water and soil and found elevated levels of aluminum in them—4,610 parts per million which are 25,000 times the safe guidelines of the WHO (World Health Organization). The entire U.S., in addition to various other NATO countries, are being sprayed.

On March 23, 2018, the Richmond County Daily Journal in Rockingham, North Carolina ran this article by Robert Lee who calls himself a concerned citizen and a U.S. Marine veteran who owns and operates Rockingham Guns and Ammo. I can relate to everything he wrote in this article and what I have witnessed since childhood.

"I'm not a conspiracy theorist, not at all. All I have to say is, it's time that I write about a subject that was brought to my attention eight years ago. When the subject of chemtrails came up, I just shrugged it off and let it go. I did not think much about it. I, of course, did from time to time see these long trails coming out of aircraft that were at a great height. They were at an altitude that was greater than any commercial aircraft I had seen flying over. Still, at the time it did not matter to me. Today it's a different story. Something is taking place and I do not believe it's a good thing.

"To start I need to go back a bit. Remember when, as children, we saw the first jet aircraft going over? It was unbelievable to say the least. It was a great sight for a child. Then the sonic boom would come from the aircraft breaking the sound barrier. I can still remember the trails of white smoke coming out, or that was what I thought it was. As it turned out, it was water vapor. These vapor trails are called contrails, which being condensation from the aircraft. Those trails lasted for but seconds as the aircraft flew over. Those trails were about 1,000 feet long or so. My point: they did not last that long at all.

"Now today things have changed. When these military aircraft come over, the trails go from horizon to horizon. One February two years ago I finally saw one of the aircraft itself. Until that day, all I had ever seen was the chemtrails and nothing more. As I sat there — and I sat there for several hours — watching what turned out to be very unnatural, I watched as these chemtrails dropped lower. As they dropped, they got wider. It was at that time that these clouds, for that is what they looked like at that point, started doing funny things. Things that normal clouds do not do. They started rolling over and twisting on to themselves. I also did take notice that the entire county had been checker-boarded in this pattern. In time, what began as a blue cloudless morning sky was no more. The whole county had a cloud over it.

"It was on that day that I did start paying more attention to these chemtrails. The government, in the beginning, stated that they had nothing to do with it. But now they have changed their story and have admitted to the spraying. One point to bring out: They say it's nothing to be concerned about. You keep on believing that. I have no trust in our government to ever tell us the truth about anything. I know firsthand just how rotten our government can be and has been in the past. We cannot trust them. To the government, we are nothing but a number to be used and abused. It happens every day and it is taking place right now as I put these words to print. Don't believe one of these written words, go outside on a cloudless day, and find out for yourself. It will be right there for you to see firsthand. Then research it and find out. I am not going to tell you that it takes place every day; still, just look. You will see regular aircraft going over and you can compare the trails.

"I can't tell you what our government is truly doing but I can say I do not believe it is for the benefit of our people. I can tell you what I have found out. Because of the persistence of the conspiracy theory and questions about government involvement, scientists and government agencies around the world have told their citizens that the chemtrails are in fact contrails.

"If that were the truth then why the patterns? Our airlines are not the ones that are doing this. It is our military.

"It depends on who you talk to and if they work for the government as to what you are told. So-called experts on atmospheric phenomena within the government will tell you chemtrails do not exist. They will tell you that the contrails are being affected by different things such as wind shear of vertical and horizontal directions. Also, they are affected by temperature, sunlight, and humidity.

"NASA, the EPA, and the FAA have stated that the checker-board look of the chemtrails is because of the patterns within the flight lanes of the commercial aircraft. The U.S. Air Force stated in a fact sheet that this has been going on from 1953 until the present day. This is another damn lie. I, just like most of you, have been looking at the sky all of my life, and never in the '60s, '70s, or '80s did I see the sky look like this. The Air Force has also stated that from the ground you cannot tell what you are looking at. I guess I have to agree with them on that point, but only if you are totally blind and live in a cave.

"Do these people really think we are that stupid? The Air Force rebutted chemtrail theories more directly and said that the theories are nothing, but a hoax and they have disproved the existence of chemtrails. They also stated that the chemtrails are nothing more than ice crystals. I can see this, maybe, on a winter day but not in July at a height of 500 feet. All this was stated in their fact sheet. The spraying seems to be more constant and the heaviest over the United States and western Europe. In Asia, Japan and Korea are being sprayed. The only country in the area that is not being sprayed at all is China. If you lean toward the conspiracy theory side, then you should not be shocked with the rest of my column. What this spraying is known as is—the genocide spraying operation.

"There have been many independent tests done over the past five years and it does not look good. It has been confirmed that all around our country a cocktail of dangerous and extremely poisonous chemicals is being dispersed. This includes barium, cadmium, nickel, mold spores, yellow fungal mycotoxins, and the best — radioactive thorium. This is not the total list. The one chemical that is being sprayed the most is aluminum. It can cause all sorts of health problems. The chemical primarily attacks the central nervous system and can cause everything from disturbed sleep, nervousness, memory loss, headaches, and emotional instability.

"With that said, have you not noticed how people have changed in recent years? We see every day more and more people dying at a very young age. Look at the mental state of people. Look at all the different drugs that we are using just to maintain our minds. One thing to add is this: Water samples on top of Mount Shasta, California have aluminum levels that are high enough to kill small rodents. The levels are off the chart with the highest being at 4,800 times the maximum contaminate level for drinking water. In a recent snow sample, the level was 100 times the level for aluminum in snow.

"Those who work in the field of geoengineering will tell you that the goal is to reduce global warming. Just another lie that we have been told. They got caught. For years, the government denied the idea of chemtrails and geoengineering. When people started to figure out what was going on, then they owned up to it. As the world's people observe more strange trails in the sky, we begin to ask more questions that the government can't answer. As we ask more questions, the world governments push justification through the mainstream media and their scientific studies."

Aluminum spraying has contributed to autism in children, increased Alzheimer's disease in the elderly, the destruction of plants, trees, fish, birds, insects, and other forms of life. Those who are involved are in a massive coverup and the operation must cost trillions or zillions of dollars.

Chemtrail sprays have gone on since the late 1990s and continue. It only stopped shortly after lockdown for the pandemic. Yesterday, October 8, 2020, the sky over Southern Nevada was covered in chemtrails all day and into the late evening, and today, the same weather pattern prevails, yet not one chemtrail in the sky. Can someone explain this to me how that can happen?

Shame on those who want to control us, harm us, and this

beautiful and very unique planet. Shame on those who continue to coverup this massive operation and claim that we are seeing only contrails in the sky, natural jet condensation. Their debunking is massive as the chemtrails and they think we are all stupid. They are complicit in tyranny against the human race and our planet.

In time, they will be stopped, and the truth will be known. As the Bible states, "Ye will know the truth, and the truth shall set you free." John 8:32.

In 2021, I foresee another year of horrible wildfires throughout the world and again in northern and southern California, Oregon and Washington, Idaho, the rainforests in Brazil and Australia. I urge any of you that live in forested areas to leave at the first sign of fires in your area. Grab only essentials and your pets and get out. The new wildfires burn hotter and faster, leaving little time to escape.

2021 Looking into The Future

CHAPTER TWELVE

THE ECONOMY

I made a startling discovery and I believe it was planned to be that way since 9-11-2001. When America was attacked September terrorists on September 11, 2001, the entire business community felt the blow. The Stock market immediately nose-dived, and almost every sector of the economy was damaged economically. The U.S. economy was already suffering through a moderate recession following the dotcom bubble, and the terrorist attacks added further injury to the struggling business community.

It was a travesty how my friends and family lost their businesses and homes.

Next came the subprime mortgage debacle from 2007 to 2010, almost ten years after 9-11. Mortgage loans were made to just about anyone, knowing most were not completely informed about the higher payments once the initial grace period ended.

As a result of the depreciating housing prices, borrowers' ability to refinance became more difficult. Borrowers found themselves unable to escape higher monthly payments by refinancing began to default.

As more borrowers stopped making their mortgage payments, foreclosures, and the supply of homes for sale increased. The banks foreclosed on many homes that set vacant for several years. This placed a downward spiral on housing prices, further lowering homeowner's equity. The decline in mortgage payments also reduced the value of mortgage-backed securities, which eroded the net worth and financial health of banks.

Stated loans or "liar loans" became as easy as getting gas at a gas station. In such a mortgage loan the borrower's income was not verified by looking at their pay stubs, W-2 forms, income tax returns, or other records. Borrows simply stated their income, and the lender took their world.

Starting in 2008, many people discovered that banks and some lenders were Robo signing for them, which lead to improper foreclosures. As many as 3.8 million people had their homes taken in foreclosures.

I kept telling my husband this was going to be a collapse in 2007. I was right. And almost ten years later, the Coronavirus hit and has put millions of people out of work and this was all planned. Trump brought back the economy from 2016 to 2019. People made huge gains with their 401K plans, the Stock Market was at its highest, and unemployment was at its lowest. How quickly some people forget the good that happened during Trump's four years in office.

Coronavirus hit the beginning of 2020, 10 years after the Mortgage Debacle. When things happen in a pattern, I realize it's not a coincidence, but a planned agenda. An estimated 163,735 small businesses have closed in the United States since March 1, 2020, and they probably will never reopen. The government has given small stimulus checks to keep people afloat, but time is running out for more Federal money. The bad news is that many people are already homeless and more will have to move out of their apartments and their homes in the months to come as COVID rages on.

If we don't get a handle on the virus with a cure, I foresee a very gloomy future for the entire world. Usually, events like this led to world wars. Can you imagine World War III fought with soldiers infected with COVID?

I don't foresee the virus ever vanishing from our planet. That's the bad news. Pandora's Box was opened upon the Earth, and this is a virus that is here to stay. It was invented to cull the herd—in other words, to remove a large number of humans from the planet.

If we can make a vaccine that will at least slow down the transmission of the virus for a while, that would help. An absolute cure won't come for at least two years.

We saw how quickly seventy-four-year-old President Donald Trump rebounded from the virus with a special 8-gram dose of an experimental antibody therapy cocktail made by the biotechnology company Regeneron. To make its monoclonal antibody therapy, Regeneron scientists selected two antibodies that best neutralized a version of the novel coronavirus in the lab. Antibodies are proteins the body makes to fight infection. The scientists copied those two antibodies to make a treatment for Covid-19.

The New York-based company confirmed that it provided the drug under a "compassionate use" request from the President's physicians but did not specify when it received the request. "There is a limited product available for compassionate use requests that have been approved under rare, exceptional circumstances on a case-by-case basis," Regeneron said in a statement. So certain people will be given this life-saving drug, but it won't be available to the general public for a while.

President Trump was being given a five-day course of the antiviral drug Remdesivir, one of the doctors treating him said during a briefing on Saturday. The treatment is intended to shorten recovery time for COVID-19 patients. This isn't a cure for COVID. He was also given the corticosteroid drug dexamethasone on Saturday after his oxygen level transiently dipped, White House physician Dr. Sean Conley said.

At this point, November 8, 2020, all new media has declared Joe Biden the new 46th president of the United States, even though ballots have not all be counted, including military votes, in most states. President Trump and his attorneys plan to file federal lawsuits against states that manipulated ballots which has been witnessed by a great number of people.

Analysts project that regardless of the victory, U.S. stock prices will be higher, even as Trump's campaign will challenge the election results in several battleground states. But I foresee a roller-coaster stock market in the coming months.

If Trump is re-elected after his court battle, stocks will rise, but under Biden's helm, it will remain high for a while, and then as Biden starts setting up his cabinet and all, we will see a very turbulent stock market. Biden will not get along with certain countries. Although real estate is going through the roof, the bubble may burst by the end of 2021.

2021 is a 5 year in numerology, and the keywords for this year will be communication, decisions, and dramatic change. It will be an unsettling year for most. Expect the unexpected.

On November 9, 2020, the New York City-based drug company Pfizer announced that they had developed a vaccine that will be 90% effective in preventing COVID-19 in participants without evidence of prior SARS-CoV-2 infection in the first interim efficacy analysis. The vaccine will be given to healthcare workers first and later to the elderly in January or February 2021 it was announced.

If Biden and Harris get elected, officially, they will probably shut down the country again with the 2nd wave of COVID coming this winter, and maybe even mandate vaccines for all. We won't have a choice.

CHAPTER THIRTEEN

THE BIOSPHERE

Indigenous people believe we are connected to everything in the world—the water, the oceans, the wind, the fire, the trees, the birds, the sea creatures, the four-legged creatures, the insects. Yet, I suspect that most of you reading this are skeptical that humans can be connected to all these living creatures. I have a cousin, now in her eighties, who is a devout Christian, believes that God does not exist in all things, and therefore, we should not pray to the elements, the animals, the birds, the sea creatures, the water. If one believes that God or the Great Spirit, Supreme Being, created all things, then that the energy is in everything around us.

The problem is that we are so disconnected from each other and all life on this planet and it shows. Our ignorance, our dogmatic beliefs, and our tunnel vision prevent us from understanding the Living Library of Earth. Indigenous people believe that when we connect and understand the symbiotic relationship with all things, we understand that all life depends on each other for Earth's balance.

The frogs, the insects, the whales, and many species tone, creating resonance to balance Earth. Resonance is sacred knowledge known and practiced by great ancient civilizations.

The Australian Aboriginals have an oral legend they have passed down through the generations that they came from a distant planet that blew up. When they arrived at Earth it was one landmass before the cataclysms. They came here to erect an energy grid to balance it.

Earth is so small that when the planet aligns in a certain way, the pull of the galactic energy is so strong that it could just suck planet Earth into the spiral plane of the galactic system and toss it around. Their planet did not have an energy grid and they knew Earth needed this to survive.

Today, Indigenous people are very concerned about the energy grids of Earth. Crystals and other minerals feed energy to the energy grid. They have been used for millions of years that way. For the health of the Earth, crystals must be free to let the energy flow to the grid.

Rare Earth minerals, gold, silver, and crystals have been removed from the Earth to such an extent that the balance is in jeopardy. Uranium, in particular, is important for this task. When it is all gone, the Earth will be completely out of balance. Australian Aboriginals have been told that every one million years, there is a seven-thousand-year-long Earth shift. Then we begin to go into a new world like we are doing now. We are seeing these events unfold before our eyes.

They say we must go into these changes and we will see a new world with heart. When we begin to understand the divinity, the cosmology of all life, we will no longer take our beautiful, and very unique planet for granted. We are the ones who will determine whether or not we will destroy our planet and ourselves. Each of us must decide whether or not to live in harmony during our lifetime and with selfless love for the benefit of all. Not only do we have this obligation for ourselves, but the future generations still unborn.

Each year scientists report on a growing number of species, animals, and insects going extinct due to over-population and pollution.

Earth biosphere exists on a symbiotic level, meaning that everything lives in harmony and when one species vanishes, it affects the whole biodiversity of Earth.

I recently watched Sir David Attenborough's documentary A Life on Our Planet, available on Netflix. David Attenborough, 94-years-old, is an English broadcaster, writer, and naturalist who has traveled around the world viewing the natural world and life that inhabits all regions of our planet.

At the beginning of the documentary, Attenborough is seen walking through the ruins of what was a thriving community near the Chernobyl nuclear plant in Ukraine. Humans haven't lived there since April 1986 when the plant exploded through human error and radiation spewed across the land. Thirty-one people died. Children are still being born with severe birth defects and rare types of cancer in the area near Chernobyl. It hasn't gone away, yet lush plants, trees, and wildlife have returned to much of the vacant land.

We are reminded of what we have done in over 70 years. In 1954 there were only 2.7 billion people on this planet. Attenborough saw oceans teeming with fish, animals abundant in the Serengeti of Africa, and lakes and rivers still pristine. Today, the Earth's population is 7.8 billion people, using up our resources at a rapid pace. Our oceans are being depleted of fish from overfishing, but in some remote places ecological practices are in use, and fish are returning.

The most troubling of our disrespect of Mother Nature is our continued use of fossil fuels that are causing our planet to rise in temperature. Glaciers are melting, giant icebergs are vanishing needed for polar bears, and the permafrost is melting, adding more methane to the atmosphere. If temperatures worldwide continue vast numbers of wildlife, insects, trees, and plant life will vanish. It's heartbreaking.

We now live in the twenty-first century and we have had years to develop natural green energy, but we don't because it would put the oil and gas industry out of business. Tesla told us about free energy available around our planet, yet we continue to harvest oil and gas through fracking, pumping toxins in the Earth to extract the oil and gas. In many areas, this has caused earthquakes. This is Mother Earth's lifeblood.

Equally upsetting is the loss of rainforests which have been clear-cut for uniform rows of oil palms planted for profit. Attenborough worries about how we are over-farming the land, but he finds hope through small successes. Sustainable farming in the Netherland has made the country one of the worldwide leaders in food exports. They take abandoned buildings and transformed each floor into rows of produce—vegetables and fruits, all protected from the weather and insect free. This is the future!

Fishing restriction around the Pacific archipelago nation of Palau enabled marine life to rebound. There is hope for our dying planet, but we can't wait any longer to make these changes. Life cycles on, and if we make the right choices now, ruin can become regrowth.

CHAPTER FOURTEEN

CORONAVIRUS
The Grinch that Stole the World

In late 2019, I had a vision about a virus like the Spanish Flu that would emerge in 2020, but at the time I couldn't fathom such a virus infecting millions and killing over one million people globally in the twenty-first century.

The Coronavirus kills indiscriminately and for some people, they have no symptoms at all—they remain asymptomatic to the disease, while others become very ill and die. It has killed all ages and all ethnic groups.

Coronavirus will never go away—it's a virus like the flu and like the flu, it will mutate from year to year. As we have already learned, vaccines have a hard time keep up with the mutations and so will the vaccines for COVID. There will be four waves of the virus into the year 2023, and perhaps longer.

Under Biden, after several months, people will begin to show disenchantment with him, especially those who voted for him. They will find that he is breaking promises, and instead of enforcing harsh laws on Coronavirus, wearing masking and revoking Executive orders made by Trump during his four years in office including rejoining the Paris Climate Accord.

Why did Trump withdraw from the Paris Climate Accord? He announced on June 1, 2017, that the U.S. would cease all participation in the 2015 Paris Agreement on climate change mitigation, and begin negotiations to re-enter the agreement "on terms that are fair to the United States, its businesses, its workers, its people, its taxpayers," or form a new agreement. Trump further stated that the "Paris accord will undermine (the U.S.) economy," and "puts the U.S. at a permanent disadvantage."

President Trump has called the Paris Agreement "job-killing" and said it would "punish the American people while enriching foreign polluters."

Biden's dementia will increase—and he will make remarks that don't make sense, there will be bursts of anger at staff and press and there will be hasty decisions made and enacted.

People who made huge gains with their 401k plans during Trump's years in office will lose considerably. Why would people gamble on Biden with his past record on the economy during the Obama year when Trump was already known to help the economy through 2019? As they say, "If it works, don't fix it."

Hard times ahead for all. Massive home foreclosures, higher unemployment with no bailouts, stock market dropping in late spring into summer 2021, suicides, and increased divorces. Shortage at grocery stores from weather and truckers going on strike. You won't like Joe Biden's world!

There's talk on the 'Stop the Tires' Facebook page, which quickly garnered 51,000 members, that a 24-hour strike could begin on Veterans Day, November 11, or possibly over the Thanksgiving holiday to shut down the industry on an important shopping and shipping weekend. They're protesting the potential of a new Green Deal under Biden or the stoppage of fracking.

If the trucker strike takes place nationwide, our grocery stores will have bare shelves again. People are angry, and they have a right to be after the election was stolen from President Trump.

We're not going to allow our freedom of election and our freedom of speech to be taken from us the socialists. The arrogant planners can't take that away from us and the Constitution of the United States.

It's time for us to begin preparing for the planned changes in earnest. All the prophecies are confusing, and many have done nothing because there are so many possibilities. Think about being prepared for any eventuality brought to us. What are your basic needs for survival—food, clothing, water.

As our arrogant planners flaunt their methodology before our eyes assuming that sleeping minds have little discernment in programming, there's no reason why we can't use this information for our advantage.

Those souls who pass away during this time sensed something huge was going to happen and many decided to observe the events from the other side and return to Earth when the dust settled and the planet is a better place to live.

2021 Looking into The Future

CHAPTER FIFTEEN

QUESTIONS AND ANSWERS

The following questions were emailed to Betsey for this book from the people who follow her daily Earth News blog. Thank you!

Question: Biden looks as if he has won even though Trump is threatening lawsuits against certain states because of ballot fraud. Do you foresee Trump getting back the extra votes and becoming re-elected?

Answer: At this moment events are changing rapidly, and anything could happen. The Hydra (a mythical serpent-like creature with many heads) exists in the New World Order that is a network covering the entire planet. These are people and businesses you'd never suspect having that much power and influence, but they do. The U.S. Senate race between Republican Senator David Perdue and Democrat Jon Ossoff in Georgia appeared to be headed for a January 2021 runoff, potentially making a pair of delayed elections that could determine control of that chamber. Only two other Senate races remain undecided. Republican Senators Thom Tillis of North Carolina and Dan Sullivan of Alaska are leading in those contests.

If Trump does get re-elected, I am sure that the remaining undecided Senate votes, will turn Democrat and the Senate and House/Congress will be run by Democrats. Can you imagine President Trump trying to get anything passed?

President-elect Biden is poised to unleash a series of executive actions on his first day in the Oval Office, prompting what is likely to be a year-long effort to unwind President Trump's domestic agenda and immediately signal a wholesale shift in the United States' place in the world.

It reminds me of the ancient Egyptian pharaoh Akhenaton who was nearly expunged from the records for his belief in one God in the forms of the Sun undoing what previous pharaohs and their many gods had taught. He created the world's first monotheistic religion and became a heretic after his death.

Question: When will the Coronavirus end?

Answer: It is with great sorrow that I don't see Coronavirus completely disappearing after being unleashed upon the Earth. That doesn't mean that it will continue to take thousands of lives. There will be vaccines, but they will need to be taken often, and with possible side effects for some. Just like the flu, each year it mutates, and new vaccines must be produced. It also hinges on the people who refuse to wear masks and not think of others. There are too many sad stories of people who had parties and someone who attended infected a large number of people who infected their families and people died.

People continue to believe the conspiracy theories that the coronavirus is a hoax, and they don't need to wear a mask because it takes away their freedom. Really? You might be one of the lucky ones who survive, but do you really want to take that chance? I don't! But perhaps I don't fully understand viruses. You will read later in the book there is a link to an interview with Dr. Steve Pieczenik and what he knows about the virus and why he won't wear a mask. He says that due to the number of obese people globally, the virus is taking a great toll on them than others who are healthier.

Of course, we are all being inconvenienced for a while, but if we come together to rid of this horrible plague, we will create a prime event where it will vanish in time like the Spanish Flu.

I still see it causing lockdowns throughout the world and the United States into 2022. There will be areas and countries that fare better than others.

Question: I heard that a vaccine will be open to the public soon. Is that another lie? Also, do you think people should give up fighting against the virus and just surrender?

Answer: Today, November 9, 2020, Pfizer drug company reported that early results of its coronavirus vaccine look promising

90% effective results in preventing COVID-19. Unfortunately, the company is on track to send to hospitals for emergency-use approval only from the Food and Drug Administration.

More vaccines will become available. Which is the best? Only time will tell after those who have volunteered to be tested with the vaccines will we know who effective it will be. Some will have adverse side effects and others will not. As fast as the virus is mutating like other flu viruses, vaccines will need to change as the virus changes. It will be an on-going struggle to stay ahead of its mutations. The second wave has already begun in many states. If Biden is elected, rumors claim he will shut down America, which will be disastrous for employees and businesses. Even martial law is rumored. If you thought Trump was a rash man, Biden is a rash man on steroids.

I foresee a huge uprising that could unite this country against Biden's draconian laws. People will revolt and it will bring about a war against the government. No, we should not give up...ever! We are "System Busters" here to create positive change.

Question: Will we be able to return to normal life soon? What will happen to children in schools?

Answer: I do not foresee a normal world for many years to come. It is a spiritual war between the Light and the Dark forces. The Family of Dark has decided it is time to take control of this planet and run it the way they want. They are in for a big surprise because anything that is out-of-balance, will need to be corrected in a big way. If humans throughout the world suddenly woke up to what is taking place and began to take charge, there would be a totally new world—the Age of Aquarius. It is up to us to make the changes now, not twenty years from now.

My heart goes out to the world's children and what they are facing in today's chaotic and out-of-balance world. Education is archaic in today's world. School books are antiquated. I was volunteering for a first-grade class in Boise, Idaho a few years ago, and I was appalled at the horrible books they were giving the future young mind. Besides being outdated, they didn't teach any uplifting lessons. I brought my children's books and they loved them. When

I was a child, we said the Pledge of Allegiance to the United States flags and sometimes we said prayers. This has all been removed from schools.

We need to help children be creative and use their imaginations. There is a future, perhaps distant, where children will learn in classrooms that are round instead of square boxes. In a round room, children will no longer feel those sitting in the front of the classroom are special. Think of King Arthur's roundtable where all the knights were equal.

Question: Will the world famine grow worse from droughts?

Answer: Yes, our world is warming each year and the planet faces greater droughts. That means greater widespread famine "of biblical proportions" due to coronavirus pandemic and extreme weather, according to the chief of the UN's food relief agency. There's only a short time to act before hundreds of millions starve. "More than 30 countries in the developing world could experience widespread famine, and in 10 of those countries there are already more than one million people on the brink of starvation," said David Beasley, executive director of the World Food Programme.

Question: 2020 has certainly been a tumultuous year. I believe that a lot of darkness is coming up so that it can be cleared from our planet. My questions are:

1. Will the corrupt politicians of the past several years be arrested and brought to justice? The Clintons in particular?
2. Will the news media become more honest?
3. Is there another, more deadly, virus that China will unleash on the world?

Answer: Arresting and prosecuting corrupt politicians would take an act of God. Trump often talked about "draining the swamp," referring to the swamp creatures (corrupt politicians) who control Washington, D.C. It would take an uprising to arrest and convict the Family of Dark for their heinous crimes against humanity. They have no remorse. The Clintons have been protected and are part of the dark cabal running our world. It will take a great cleansing of our planet to remove these dark characters from the planet, and that might entail a lot of the Family of Light passing as well.

Will the news media become more honest? Not in your lifetime. Most of the major networks are owned by The Family of Dark. The Washington Post is owned by Jeff Bezos who owns the monopoly company Amazon and is one of the richest men in the world. The tentacles of these people or cabal go everywhere and enshroud the world with their immorality and control of our world.

I do not foresee another more deadly virus at this time—perhaps in 2027. A nuclear plant disaster would be more likely to happen. Fukushima is still a major concern for Japan and a huge earthquake hitting that region could happen again in 2021. Another nuclear disaster could be looming in the future. Japan is one of the most active earthquake regions in the world.

Question: I have a question for your new book. What will happen with Nibiru (aka Planet X)? I've read on Zeta Talk about how awful things will be and since I live in California, I would like to know what you predict.

Answer: Planet X aka Nibiru does exist and in 2016 two Caltech scientists, Brown and Batygin, had a press conference and claimed to have found the 9th planet or Planet X. The story was quickly downplayed by NASA and the press. What else is new—they are always suppressing the truth.

People have photographed Planet X and its moons around the setting sun. Our extreme weather is due in part to Planet X's gravitational pull on the Earth. It is believed to be the size of Jupiter.

Recently NASA announced it is monitoring a strange anomaly in Earth's magnetic field: a giant region of lower magnetic intensity in the atmosphere above the planet, stretching out between South America and southwest Africa. This vast, developing phenomenon, called the South Atlantic Anomaly, has intrigued and concerned scientists. The space agency's satellites, and the space station are particularly vulnerable to the weakened magnetic field. It's a kind of 'pothole in space' —which doesn't affect life on Earth, but it does in our ISS (International Space Station), which has to pass directly through the anomaly as they loop around the planet at low-Earth orbit altitudes.

I do believe Nibiru is currently passing through our solar system and bringing lots of debris with it—meteor and bolides, and even a few asteroids. Watch the skies—2021 will be a sky of fireworks. Depending on how close it comes to Earth during its passage will depend on how great the Earth changes become. If my dreams at the age of seven become reality we can expect cataclysmic Earth changes—volcanoes erupting worldwide including dormant ones, powerful earthquakes 9+ magnitude, tsunamis, and mountain building in some areas.

If you decide to move, seek older geologic areas, places that aren't known for big earthquake faults. Areas of the Southwest are good and most of central Canada will be unaffected by some of the changes. Be mindful to live at least 100 miles inland from the ocean waters.

Question: Some astrologers say that if the Nov. 3 election had been delayed, the results came out on the same day, then President Trump would lose the election. In case if voting or polling results were to get delayed by 4 to 8 weeks, then Trump will get re-elected. It may be a repeat of the Presidential Election between George W. Bush and Al Gore that happened on November 7, 2000. The election results were withheld for around 5 weeks as it was too close to call in the State of Florida. Of course, the Bush cabal won. Any chance Trump can win?

Answer: At this time the new media and press announced Biden had won the Electoral votes. Trump refuses to concede, knowing he was cheated out of a fair election. According to the press and I don't buy half of what they dish out to us that claimed Melania Trump and Jared Kushner, Trump's son-in-law, have urged him to concede. President Trump is a fighter and doesn't give up easily. He's a smart man and has some surprises for America. He does what he wants to do and always has. Trump will not concede to Biden until the Courts decide against him, which couldn't happen considering the corruption in this country at this time. The Democrats and elite have tried everything to get rid of him in the past four years—Russia probe, impeachment, and nothing worked. The Family is Light is on Trump's side, believe it or not! The left will pull out all the stops to get him buried one way or another.

Question: Are the major network news stations NBC, CBS, CNN, and ABC, all corrupt?

Answer: They are all owned by huge corporations that dictate what they want on the news. News doesn't care about the truth; they want sensational news that gets you to tune into their network every night. The new media has become tabloid news like the National Enquirer. They will do anything to get ratings and even embellish the news. Their motto is, "If it bleeds, it leads." Have you noticed how the news has been all about COVID, while other stories never make the nightly news? Now it's all about Trump and how he won't concede and he's harming America, and how Biden, Mr. Superman, is going to save the day by stopping COVID and reversing most of Trump's executive orders. Can you say propaganda and mind-control of the masses? Biden has pledged to abandon Mr. Trump's travel ban on mostly Muslim countries and to begin calling foreign leaders in an attempt to restore trust among the United States' closest allies. Watch the terrorists flood into the United States!

Fox News on November 9th cut off President Trump's press secretary, Kayleigh McEnany, as she discussed voter fraud in the election. If that would have been one of Biden's people, she would not have been cut off from the press conference. Is that fair?

Question: Will people who voted for Trump be targeted?

Answer: I am sure this will happen in the workplace across America and heavily on social media. People will not want to become targets for malice. I have already received some angry Biden supporter's emails who still have to harass others even though it appears Biden won. You'd think they'd be happy about the results, but they still have to be bullies. Our freedom of speech will become a thing of the past if Biden is confirmed.

On October 25, 2019, Representative Alexandria Ocasio-Cortez, a member of the Democratic Socialists of America, has fully embraced the demand by the US intelligence agencies that technology monopolies censor political speech on the internet. At a hearing recently at the House Financial Services Committee, Alexandria Ocasio-Cortez called on Facebook CEO Mark Zuckerberg to "take down lies." And Facebook has and Twitter puts up disclaimers on all of Trump's information and YouTube recently was temporarily blacked-out for any Trump-related information.

Questions: What do you foresee for the world's spiritual leaders—The Dalai Lama, South Africa's spiritual leader Desmond Tutu, and Pope Francis who have all reached their 80s? Do you foresee any one of them dying in 2021?

Answer: His Holiness the 14th Dalai Lama, now 85-years-old, and Desmond Tutu, 89-years-old, are spiritual friends and have spent much time together. They have a deep respect for each other and are kindred souls. If one leaves, the other will follow shortly. A book titled, *The Wisdom of Forgiveness* © 2004, tells of their long-lasting friendship. A wonderful book. Pope Francis turns 84-years-old on December 17, 2020. I do see the Pope living several more years, but the Dalai Lama could leave us. His vibration rate is down, and I have read of his health issues as well as Desmond Tutu's declining health. We will lose two great leaders. The Dalai Lama has said the role (reincarnation) will one day end. Better to have no Dalai Lama than "a stupid one," he said. He has indicated that he does not want to reincarnate as a Lama again.

Unfortunately, I do not foresee the current Dalai Lama returning to his dear homeland of Tibet.

Question: Worldwide there are sightings of orbs that shapeshift into a solid craft and the sightings are increasing. Are they benevolent or the not so nice aliens?

Answer: Both and some of our military. We have several types of aliens/beings that are here, and some that have bases deep in the oceans, lakes, and in deep underground bases. Some are benevolent, but the reptilian race is an advanced species but unevolved spiritually. Please refer to my new book, *Extraterrestrial Encounters of The Extraordinary Kind,* available on Amazon in softcover and Kindle e-book. I have researched and written about many types of aliens, their agenda for us and Earth, both benevolent and malevolent. We will have proof of aliens soon when disclosure is leaked by certain high officials.

Question: President Trump fired the Secretary of Defense Mark Esper and gave the title to Christopher Miller, the current director of the National Counterterrorism Center. What's with that?

Answer: It appears that President Trump fired Esper after he said he did "not support involving the Insurrection Act," amide nationwide protests over the summer months.

Question: I once read that people would live to be 200 years old. And my first thought was who would want to live that long. But I have heard mention of med beds. These beds would cure people of illnesses and cancers and that hospitals would close, which is another prediction you mentioned about hospitals. I'm fascinated by these predictions and hope you wouldn't think I'm in left field here. Keep up the great work and I'll keep on reading.

Answer: Thank you for your excellent questions, but I don't recall ever posting anything about any Med Bed ET technology. Med Beds seem to apply to two different technologies. One is a bed that can keep the Coronavirus patient sitting upright and making it easier to breathe. The other applies to holographic medical pods and given to us by extraterrestrials. There is a YouTube video about a medical pod, however, the video is in Italian. I did find this information on the internet:

MED BEDS (Holographic Medical Pods) - One of Many Healing Technologies Expected to Come Forward Upon Disclosure Med Bed technology has been "suppressed" and hidden from the public for a long, long time. Fortunately, due to the planetary shift from 3D to 5D. As far as I know and sense, this is not true.

Med Beds is a technology that has been given to humanity by off-world Extraterrestrials. A Med Bed is based on tachyon particle energy and plasma (plasmatic) energy. The soil, the atmosphere, the water, everything is plasma energy, everything in the universe is plasma energy, it's just a different form through vibrational frequency.

Your question about human life expectancy going to 200 years, seems impossible, but Methuselah lived 900 years according to the Bible, and Pharaoh Ramses lived to be 96 over 3,000 years ago. It is believed that some extraterrestrials have the ability to live a thousand years. In the next 50 to 100 years, humans will live well over 100 years of age. It is believed by scientists that the oxygen levels on Earth were much greater, and that enabled humans to live longer.

Certainly, living longer would bring about many concerns— staying gainfully employed to support such a long life, marriage, children, legal and ethical questions. Would longevity be a blessing or a curse. We live and die and as spiritualists believe we are reincarnated into another body, which sounds more exciting. New adventures, new relationships, old ones renewed, new soul lessons

Question: I live in Canada and I am worried that we are going through what is happening in the U.S. We were told that to offset what was essential, and economic collapse on an international scale is coming, that the federal government was going offer Canadians a total debt relief. The federal government will offer to eliminate all personal debts with all funding provided to Canada by the IMF under what is known as the "World Debt Reset Program." In exchange for acceptance of this total debt forgiveness, the induvial will forever forfeit ownership of any and all property and assets.

Furthermore, the individual would have to agree to partake in the COVID 19 and COVID 21 vaccination schedule, which would provide the individual with unrestricted travel and unrestricted living even under a full lockdown; through the use of photo identification referred to as Canada's Health Pass.

The World Bank and the IMF have been pressing the G20 group of leading developing and developed nations to extend the debt suspension initiative for a further 12-month period while a long-term plan is worked out. A bad debt write-off is an accounting method that makes it possible to remove or write-off a debt that has been deemed to be uncollectable.

Answer: I wish there was better news, but no government is going to relieve us of our debts. Never. How could they do this when most countries have a huge deficit. This sounds like the NESARA myth for Canada—all debt will be paid with one big caveat—give your life to them and become their slaves.

Question: Will we know more about Jeffery Epstein's sex trafficking business and the people involved? Will Prince Andrew and Bill Clinton be exposed? Will Espstein's accomplice, Ghislaine Maxwell, 58, be convicted on July 12, 2021, in her court case?

Answer: The rabbit hole goes deep, and many world-renowned people are involved in satanic rituals and human trafficking throughout the world and this includes children. Recently it was revealed that Billionaire Bill Gates met with Jeffrey Epstein on several occasions.

Ghislaine Maxwell pleaded not guilty to charges on six counts, including transportation of a minor with intent to engage in criminal sexual activity. She also faces perjury charges for statements she made during a deposition in 2016 about her role in Mr. Epsteins's alleged sex trafficking operations. She is considered a flight risk, but I suspect that she will never have a court hearing and end up dead like Epstein, and again the report will read, "suicide." Those involved in his trafficking of adults and children, don't want their names exposed and will do anything to silence those who want to her talking.

I can guarantee Jeffrey Epstein did not commit suicide. He was murdered to stop him from revealing the powerful men who were connected to him. Even Joe Biden's son, Hunter Biden appears to have had some connection in human trafficking. Bill Clinton and Hillary Clinton are involved in nefarious dealings. I won't go into it here, but you can read about all the people who died under mysterious circumstances while Bill Clinton was President from 1993 to 2001. I suggest you read the book, *Trance Formation of America,* by Cathy O'Brien about her sexual abuse as an MK-Ultra mind-controlled slave by former President George H.W. Bush, Dick Cheney and even Hillary's name is mentioned.

Will we ever learn the truth? These powerful people will never allow their dirty secrets to be revealed. It will never happen because the Family of Dark includes very powerful people, you'd never suspect of being involved in human trafficking and child pornography, but they are.

Misuse of secularity is nothing new. It goes back hundreds of years. We hide from the truth of the matter. We continue to hear of Catholic priests sexually abusing young boys and girls, yet the pious turn their backs on this. I recently gave a reading to a young man that confided to me that he had a sexual encounter at eighteen with a Catholic priest who was beloved by his parish. He was later found to be guilty and discharged as a priest, but never imprisoned for his abuse of young underaged boys.

We are about to learn that many leaders from around the globe, especially in the fields of politics, religion, and education that are dedicated to children, are part of a massive covert organization of pedophiles who use children in horrible ways. This is one of the darkest secrets of the Family of Dark in our world. The houses of the rich are full of stories of abuse from one generation to the next, sex for satanic ritual, and for calling in the darkness, where there is no love, only the vibration of power.

Perhaps as we examine the dark misuse in our world and how we have been tricked and manipulated by these people, we will reevaluate our values as spiritual beings. It's time to tell our children about the perversions of religion, king and queens, and our leaders.

Angry protests will arise from people around the world, and the energies will intensify as we are asked to change and open our eyes to what is real and what is not. We will pull back the curtain to see the Family of Dark isn't as powerful as they believe. In 2021, there will be shocking news, revelations, and scandals the like we have never seen before. You are probably wondering how things became so corrupt? It's because we didn't want to open our eyes to the corruption and so it has proliferated. The people involved were abused themselves and they continue their abuse of others in the name of the dark vibration that enshrouds our world.

One such person who tried to awaken us was Father Malachi Martin, an Irish Catholic priest and controversial author, born July 23, 1921, and died July 27, 1999. He was originally ordained as a Jesuit priest and became Professor of Paleontology at the Vatican's Pontifical Biblical Institute, and from 1958 he served as a theological adviser to Cardinal Augustin Bea during the preparations for the Second Vatican Council. Through the years he became disillusioned by reforms in the Church and renounced his vows in 1964, moving to New York City. His 17 novels and non-fiction books were often critical of the Catholic Church. He believed the Church should have disclosed the third secret of Fatima, Portugal as the Virgin Mary had requested. Two of his books, *The Scribal Character of The Dead Sea Scrolls*, 1958, and *Hostage to the Devil,* 1976, dealt with Satanism, demonic possession, and exorcism.

He knew that the pedophile priests in the Catholic Church were not being dealt with and often protected from their horrible crimes against children.

Father Malachi Martin's Accusations
Father Malachi Martin said, "Anybody who is acquainted with the state of affairs in the Vatican in the last 35 years is well aware that the Prince of Darkness has had and still has his surrogates in the court of Saint Peter in Rome."

From 1958 until 1964, Jesuit priest Martin served in Rome where he was a close associate of the renowned Jesuit Cardinal Augustin Bea and the Pope. Released afterward from his vows of poverty and obedience at his own request (but as a priest), Father Martin moved to New York and became a best-selling writer of fiction and non-fiction. He often made references to satanic rites held in Rome in his 1990 non-fiction best-seller, The Keys of This Blood, in which he wrote: "Most frighteningly for Pope John Paul

[II], he had come up against the irremovable presence of a malign strength in his own Vatican and certain bishops' chanceries. It was what knowledgeable Churchmen called the 'superforce.'

Rumors, always difficult to verify, tied its installation to the beginning of Pope Paul VI's reign in 1963. Indeed, Paul had alluded somberly to 'the smoke of Satan which has entered the Sanctuary'. . . an oblique reference to an enthronement ceremony by Satanists in the Vatican. Besides, the incidence of Satanic pedophilia—rites and practices— was already documented among certain bishops and priests as widely dispersed as Turin, in Italy, and South Carolina, in the United States. The cultic acts of Satanic pedophilia are considered by professionals to be the culmination of the Fallen Archangel's rites."

Father Martin said, "Satanism is all around us. We deny it at our peril. I could point out places only minutes from here [New York City] where black masses are being celebrated. I know of cases of human sacrifice—the sacrifice of babies. I know the people who are doing these things."

The Mysterious Death of Justice Antonin Scalia

From the moment I heard about Justice Antonin Scalia's death on February 13, 2016 (13 is an Illuminati number, at age 79, I suspected murder. (Learn more about the power of number 13 in my book Mystic Revelations of Thirteen).

The owner of the ranch claimed he found Scalia with a pillow over his face. That doesn't sound like a natural death. On Thursday, February 25, 2016, the Washington Post reported that U.S. Justice Antonin Scalia spent his last hours with members of a secretive society of elite hunters at a West Texas ranch. The exclusive fraternity for hunters is called the International Order of St. Hubertus, an Austrian society that dates back to the 1600s. This society was founded in Bohemia in 1695 by Count Franz Anton von Sporck, which is now in the modern-day Czech Republic.

Besides the ranch owner stating Scalia had a pillow "over his head," this detailed with the fact that a physician had declared him dead over the phone and the family didn't want an autopsy. This prompted speculation about foul play and the "obvious" role of the Obama administration in Scalia's "untimely" death.

On "Trunews," End Times, radio host Rick Wiles discussed "the possible occult connections" to the death of Justice Scalia Wiles explained that the "Luciferian" "devil-worshipers" who control the government are out for blood, noting that Lupercalia is observed between February 13 and 15. Scalia's body was discovered on the 13th. "There's always human sacrifice involved," he said.

There's a clandestine club called the Bohemian Club in San Francisco, which is associated with the all-male occult Bohemian Grove, also a secret club located in Sonoma county—Russian River area. The Bohemian Club has seen the likes of former President George H.W. Bush, a member, and reportedly Dick Cheney and Bill Clinton were participants. Strange rituals take place there. The Bohemian Grove is a 2,700-acre virgin redwood grove in Northern California, 75 miles north of San Francisco, where the rich, the powerful, and their entourage visit with each other during the last two weeks of July while camping out in cabins and tents and performing strange occult rituals.

It was in 1`995 that I discovered the shocking book Trance-Formation of America by Cathy O'Brien and Mark Phillips about children who have been abducted for mind-control experiments and other horrible occult rituals by the CIA. Cathy O'Brien was taken as a child and endured horrible physiological and sexual abuse. It was all part of the Central Intelligence Agency's MK-Ultra Project Monarch mind-control operation. The most shocking information was about the people involved—Dick Cheney, Bill and Hillary Clinton, and George H.W. Bush. The repeated sexual assault on children and even games where children were hunted like animals on a hunting ranch in California is too frightening to fathom. The book has been dismissed by some as pure fantasy, yet it makes you wonder about Scalia's mysterious death and connection to an elite society linked to occult practices (i.e. Jeffrey Epstein's link to the famous). Cathy and Mark say the sexual and satanic rituals are so widespread it involves clergy, justices, law enforcement, and politicians.

Isn't it time we had our eyes wide open to the darkness that invades our world so we can transform the anger, hate, and abuse into love, light, and forgiveness? Much healing needs to take place on our planet if we are to survive and evolve.

Question: Could you include some predictions for Canada in your upcoming 2021 predictions book. Will PM Justin Trudeau remain as Prime Minister for many more years; Trudeau has broken many ethical laws and lies to the voters; where is Canada Heading forward in terms of becoming a Marxist country with Trudeau or the liberals ruling; will any conservative leader defeat the liberals; and other predictions for our Country.

Answer: I don't know much about Canada's laws or about Prime Minister Justin Trudeau, (48-years-old) who was re-elected in 2019, and how people feel about the son of former Prime minister Pierre Trudeau. He legalized cannabis for Canada and says he supports feminist issues, but was chastised as a bigot, and he has had recent death threats. A controversial event was held on Parliament Hill known as the "United We Roll" truck convoy, at which several members of the far-right yellow vests movement shouted slogans and carried signs calling for Trudeau to be hanged for "treason." From what little I have read, it sounds as if Canada is experiencing much of what we are in this country. People seem dissatisfied with their government worldwide and more will be taking to the streets to protest. I foresee more protests becoming violent in 2021.

Question: if Betelgeuse goes supernova what we can expect to see on Earth?

Answer Betelgeuse goes supernova, this is what we will observe on Earth. "All this brightness would be concentrated into one point," Howell says. "So, it would be this incredibly intense beacon in the sky that would cast shadows at night, and that you could see during the daytime. Everyone all over the world would be curious about it because it would be unavoidable." Humans would be able to see the supernova in the daytime sky for roughly a year, he says. And it would be visible at night with the naked eye for several years, as the supernova aftermath dims. "By the time it fades completely, Orion will be missing its left shoulder," adds

Sarafina Nance, a University of California, Berkeley, a graduate student who's published several studies of Betelgeuse. It would also affect animals and their night navigation.

Article by Will Dunham: Astronomers have determined the cause of the dramatic dimming observed last year and earlier this year of one of the brightest stars in the night sky, a colossus called Betelgeuse that appears to be on its way toward a violent death. Based on Hubble Space Telescope observations, scientists said they believe Betelgeuse ejected a huge hot, dense cloud of material into space that cooled to form dust, shielding the star's light and making it appear dimmer from the perspective of viewers on Earth. "Frankly, we don't know for sure how soon Betelgeuse will go supernova," astrophysicist Andrea Dupree, director of the Solar Stellar Planetary Sciences Division at the Harvard-Smithsonian Center for Astrophysics and leader of the research published this week in the Astrophysical Journal, said on Friday.

Question: I fear more suicides coming from people giving up about COVID, and probably more murders? What do you see?

Answer: If the economy continues its downward trend and unemployment doesn't rebound, there will be more suicides and murders. Some people believe suicide means eternal hell and no redemption, but they are completely wrong. Suicides do not have any particular punishment, except for the soul's choosing. You see, we judge ourselves after we die. Many people who have experienced a near-death experience, recall a life review, where everything they have done, both good and bad, is shown to them. However, any problems and unlearned lessons that were not faced in this life will be met in another lifetime. There are different reasons for suicide—terminal illness, constant physical or mental pain, mental illness, and those unable to face their problems, which is the hardest lesson for the soul. Escaping life's problems, no matter how harsh, is being selfish, and usually results in the soul sleeping for a long time before reincarnating or spending many lifetimes resolving their action against the godly temple—the body.

If a person kills himself believing that the act will destroy his consciousness forever, this person is in for a big surprise and this could severely impede his or her soul's progress.

God does not judge us, so it is the soul's duty to either find forgiveness in self or torture themselves in their own created hell. And guess what, there is no hell or devil—the church long ago created these mythical places and evil beings to control their flocks. There are lower entities that do cause problems for us in the physical world from time to time.

If you believe that you will experience hell when you die, you will have created that experience from your thoughts. When you die, you become pure energy and pure thought and whatever you think becomes an instant reality.

Those who die accidentally or from an accidental drug overdose will find faster forgiveness for their actions than those who run from their problems and commit this act. Prayers, love, and forgiveness are always needed for these souls.

Spirit guides rush in to assist those who have committed suicide, so the soul is never alone. There are various therapies used to heal the soul. For example, the personality may be led back to the events prior to the decision. Then the personality is allowed to change the decision of suicide—a type of movie redone. An amnesia effect is induced so the suicide itself is forgotten. Only later is the individual informed of the act when the soul is better able to face it and understand its actions.

Sometimes the personality refuses to accept death. The individual knows quite well that it is dead but refuses to complete the psychic separate from the physical body to spirit.

Some souls refuse to leave their earthly existence and remain trapped in an in-between world and wander perhaps bewildered through his homes or surroundings. These we call ghosts.

Unfortunately, there are a huge number of limbo souls trapped in this reality, and someday when humans have learned how to clear the ethereal band surrounding Earth, these lost souls will be released from their self-created prison.

Those who understand thoroughly that reality is self-created will have the least difficulty on the Other Side. Those who have learned to understand and operate in the mechanics of the dream state will have a great advantage. A belief in demons is highly disadvantageous after death, as it is during physical existence. A systematized theology of the opposite is also detrimental. If you believe, for example, that all good must be balanced by evil, then you bind yourself into a system of reality that is highly limiting, and that contains within it the seed of great torment.

Question: Do you foresee Melania Trump leaving Donald if he loses his fight to be re-elected? There are rumors that she plans to divorce him.

Answer: Melania Trump has been unhappy in the marriage for a long time but promised not to leave until he was no longer president. I am sure that a divorce is inevitable.

Question: I have a question about what is your views of the LGBTQ community and do you think that Trump's new Supreme Court Justice pick Ann Bennett is not a good choice?

Answer: This is the twenty-first century and we still haven't learned to love one another no matter what their color, religion, or sexual preference happens to be. We are all God's children. As the Bible says, *judge not, lest ye be judged.* Here on Earth, we take on physical bodies but, in the afterlife, we are neither male nor female. God does not judge anyone. Everyone has a right to be here. When we despise someone, we despise God and ourselves, because we were created in his mind. We humans believe we are self-righteous because of programming from religion and previous generations, be we are all equal in God's eyes. The reason many souls chose to return as gay or lesbian is that it's a lesson for humans that all souls matter in God's eyes. No one is better than another—we are equal in God's eyes.

Amy Coney Barrett will be a good justice. I don't foresee Roe vs Wade law being overturned in the Supreme Court. Roe v. Wade, 410 U.S. 113, was a landmark decision of the U.S. Supreme Court in which the Court ruled that the Constitution of the United States protects a pregnant woman's liberty to choose to have an abortion without excessive government restriction

Questions: Do you foresee nurses and doctors walking out due to the masses converging on hospitals again with COVID?

Answer: Salt Lake City, Utah, and other parts of Utah, Idaho, and New York City are experiencing a second wave of COVID patients. Seriously ill COVID-19 patients are starting to fill up hospital beds in record numbers, and health care workers are bracing for even more patients to come in the wake of skyrocketing coronavirus infections again. Healthcare workers are already overworked, and they may walk out.

As of Wednesday, nearly 62,000 COVID-19 patients were hospitalized around the country, surpassing the highs of the midsummer and spring surges. This is double the numbers of hospitalized as of late September.

It will get worse, much worse. And of course, Biden will blame it all on Trump when most of these states would not enforce masks like Utah and parts of Idaho.

Question: What will happen to social media? People are fed up with all the censorship lately—we no longer have any freedom of speech.

Answer: We are treated like a communist country. What happened to freedom of speech in America? I understand blocking terrorist threats, but we have rights. Facebook and Twitter have blocked Trump, but do you think they would block Biden? That would be a cold day in hell! Many people are coming together to leave Facebook, and hopefully, we can find alternate ways of communicating with each other and not be censored. We are the people who support social media, and yet they don't care about us.

Question: The amount spent on both the presidential and congressional campaigns will hit nearly $14 billion, according to the nonpartisan Center for Responsive Politics, breaking all records for the 2020 election. This money could have been used to help those unemployed, instead of sinking money into ads. Will this ever change?

Answer: Joe Biden raised $364.5 million in August for his campaign and his joint committees with the Democratic Party. This is unconscionable that this much money is spent to help raise money for an election and on election ads. Super Pacs have been allowed to sway elections with their power and money, and that's not fair.

We cling to outdated ideologies and laws and that must be changed.

Question: Do you foresee a world war in the next few years?

Answer: Since timelines are changing, it depends on who becomes our next president. War could happen in the next three years and nuclear weapons used. Biden plans to play footsies again with Iran. Biden and Obama secretly organized an airlift of $400 million worth of cash to Iran that coincided with the January release of four Americans detained in Tehran, according to U.S. and European officials and congressional staff briefed on the operation afterward. Can you guess what the Iranians did with the $400 million in cash? Nuclear weapons development.

Question: You interviewed Betty Andreasson Luca and her husband Bob Luca about their abductions through the years by the gray aliens and the human-looking elders. Was Betty or Bob given a message about the fate of humanity?

Answer: Raymond Fowler wrote the book *The Watchers* and detailed the Luca's abduction. Of all the alien abductee stories, their story is detailed and offers many unanswered questions as to why the aliens abduct certain people. Betty and Bob are religious people and Betty continues to believe her abductors were angelic. Betty was told by the aliens that they are "The Watchers" of humanity and our planet. They are preserving our genetic material because the human race will become sterile by pollution, viruses, and bacteria. They are creating human-alien hybrids.

Bob Luca under hypnosis said this, "You see, the body is the shell…the real you is the light person inside, and that part never dies." We advance through stages. This process, he said, the human mind is unable to comprehend just as it is unable to comprehend the endlessness of the universe in space. It is a never-ending process. It will always be and has always been. He continued, "The future is not to be known by us but is given at times when deemed proper. It is the decision of the Elders (human-looking aliens), who watch over us, make the decision and help us if necessary." When a person is faced with possible death, and their time isn't up, a personal warning is given into that future event. "The message may be to only one or two people—to listen, to believe—and for that reason, all through the course of their life, by not being in that place at that time or whatever…they may complete their life cycle in the manner that they are supposed to. Accidents do happen, but yet those who have a destiny to fulfill—they will be given a way out to avoid a bad situation such as not getting on an airplane that will crash, not being in a town where an earthquake is about to happen, not being on a boat that will sink. In these cases, a glimpse of the future is given for a specific person, and not for all."

Bob was told, "We are all constantly being monitored. Nothing that you do in your life escapes them. It's like a recorder. Your life, your existence on the Earth plane, is all recorded from the time you were born until the time you die; everything is there. How you react, what you do during your life. Even your innermost thoughts, feeling, and emotions (are recorded). It's all part of the process. This process determines how rapidly you will advance and what your next step or phase will be, what teaching you need to receive, what hardship you must undergo to deepen your understanding. It's all record."

Bob added this, "Everything in nature has a plus and a minus, a light and a dark, a negative and positive, a good and a bad. It must be, for without some content of evil (in our world), there will be no good. There can be no growth."

If all the souls on the planet knew this spiritual information and live their lives in accordance with the spiritual and universal laws, we would live in a utopian world, and not the world we presently live in.

Bob was asked by the hypnotist if evil will always exist. "There will come a time when evil will be wiped away. That time is not close at hand. When the time comes, our growth will not cease. Rather, we will advance into further planes of existence. Right now, the type of society that is not possible because the people of this plane as a whole are not very advanced spiritually. Technology is advancing. Spirituality, unfortunately, is not keeping pace. Man is developing many things that are harmful to him, which he does not understand. Man (humans) need spiritual growth badly."

Question: I have a few questions. One of your predictions (may have been last year) you mentioned Trump would erase the debt. You didn't see how it could happen. Could this be the Gesara/Nesara? I see on your Earth News that it was a hoax.

Answer: I don't foresee the government ever forgiving our debts and taxes. It was rumored for a while that President Trump was going to reinstate the Gold Standard, but in today's world, it's doubtful that would work. The gold standard is a monetary system where a country's currency or paper money has a value directly linked to gold. Trump never mentioned anything about the Gold Standard.

In the mid-1990s, my long-time friend Janey told me about NESARA (National Economic Security and Recovery Act, and how all debts would be canceled, and the IRS would cease to exist. I told her, "no way will that ever happen." She wasn't going to hear any negative input about NESARA from me and held onto the belief.

Now that 2020 has arrived, there are still people who believe the government would cancel all our debts. Maybe in another reality but not this one.

NESARA was the brainchild of Harvey Francis Barnard who claimed that the proposals, which included replacing the income tax with a national sales tax, abolishing compound interest on secured loans, and returning to a bimetallic currency, that would result in 0% inflation and creating a more stable economy. The proposals were never introduced before Congress, but the NESARA legend lived on due to a woman named Shaini Candace Goodwin, doing business under the name of "Dove of Oneness." She claimed the act was passed with additional provisions, but it was suppressed by George W. Bush's administration and the Supreme Court.

Goodwin eventually started her website, "Dove of Oneness" and began posting her forums. It was later revealed that she was part of the cult group, The Ramtha School of Enlightenment.

Her website also claimed the NESARA bill floated around Congress before finally being passed by a secret session in March 2000 and signed by President Bill Clinton. It further claimed that the new law was to begin at 10 a.m. on September 11, 2001, but the computers and the data of the beneficiaries of the trillions of dollars of "Prosperity Fund" were destroyed on the second floor of the World Trade Center towers in New York City during the supposed terrorist attacks.

I doubt this happened, but it does make a nice story. Also, it was stated that an earlier gag order was issued by the Supreme Court which prohibited any official or private source from discussing it, under penalty of death. She referred to the "White Knights" a group of high-ranking military officials who have since been struggling to have the law enacted despite opposition from President George W. Bush. Goodwin believed that Bush and his cronies orchestrated the September 11 attacks and the Iraq War as distractions from NESARA. She often claimed that Bush officials were attempting to hack into her site and to prevent her from publicizing the law.

Question: What do you think about the 9-11 events in 2001 when the Trade Towers were supposedly hit by commercial planes? Do you believe our government was involved?

Answer: In 2000, I had a vivid vision that there was a covert operation by certain people in our government (I know who, but darn not say) who contributed to the destruction of the World Trade Towers for their own gain. There are too many videos that have been posted on YouTube showing that what appeared to be an implosion brought down building 7 and the second building. It was an implosion.

Josh Good lived in an apartment near the Trade Towers on September 11, 2001. He captured what happened that day and the 2nd Trade Building was not hit by a plane as we were told. Josh wrote: "I recorded on 9/11/2001 from the roof of my apartment on the corner of Fulton Street and William Street, and then continues on the street going towards the WTC on Fulton Street. The video begins as I ran onto the roof of my apartment building and continues until right before the 1st building came down. I was standing 1 block away." Here is a YouTube video link that proves a plane never hit the second building, which may not remain on YouTube.

https://www.youtube.com/watch?time_continue=1815&v=siYkDNb eRZk&feature=emb_logo

I have always known that our own government committed this heinous crime against humanity that killed 2,977 people that day. In a symbolic dream in 2000, I was shown a huge apple tree full of beautiful apples. Suddenly the leaves and apples began to fall and then the entire tree was sucked into the ground and vanished. At the time I didn't under the symbology of the giant apple tree—it was New York City, known as the "Big Apple" and the leaves were papers flying from the towers and the apples falling from the giant tree were humans jumping from the buildings.

I wish that I could describe the horrific events I was shown in a vision before the plane or planes crashed into the Trade buildings, but you'd never believe me. You'd tell me that our dear, sweet government or military would never do such heinous things to humans. Think again. They've committed experiments on U.S. citizens without their permission as far back as the 1940s.

This act of treason against the United States orchestrated by evil people in our government should have been brought to trial like the Nazis at the Nuremberg Trial after World War II. Some of the people involved have died and remain in the afterlife in a very dark place. Some of the plotters are alive and will never be brought to trial.

Not only have we been lied to about the events of 9-11, but many other events like TWA Flight 800 that exploded 12 minutes after takeoff from JFK International Airport in Queens, New York at 8:31 pm EDT on July 17, 1996.

Countless witnesses watched a missile hit the aircraft and explode it. After the investigations, physical and observational data were absent from official reports.

My nephew was serving the Navy in 1996 and heard that it was a missile launch from a Naval ship off the coast that was testing its live ordinance and the missile test went awry. On June 19, 2013, a documentary presented evidence the government investigation into the crash was a cover-up that made national news headlines with statements from six members of the original investigation team, now retired, who also filed a petition to reopen the probe. The other theory was a terrorist missile strike.

Question: Is the QAnon theory true?

Answer: Trump has mentioned draining the swamp in Washington, D.C. He has always been aware of the Family of Dark or Elite or New World Order who has their claws in everything— the news media, the entertainment business, and just about every other business. Think of them as the World Mafia. A spiritual war is about to take place—the Light against the Dark.

QAnon is a far-right conspiracy theory. It alleges that a cabal of Satan-worshiping pedophiles is running a global child sex-trafficking ring and plotting against U.S. President Donald Trump, who has battled against the cabal. Explaining the "big tent conspiracy theory" that falsely claims that President Trump is facing down a shadowy cabal of Democratic pedophiles.

QAnon is right about a global child and human trafficking ring connected to powerful people and leaders involved in dark, occult practices. Jeffrey Epstein, who was involved in trafficking underaged girls, was also conducting satanic rituals in his Caribbean Island hideaway with powerful men and a few women.

When Epstein was alive, Little Saint James had nicknames like "The Island of Sin", "Pedophile Island", and "Orgy Island". These nicknames alone are giant red flags. Meanwhile, Epstein often called it "Little Saint Jeff's."

Epstein had an Egyptian temple on his private island in the U.S. Virgin Islands and although there are no photographs of the inside, I have remote viewed satanic alters inside. Epstein was murdered to stop him from naming important and well-known people that visited his island of sex. Horrible things went on there.

Question: I own a cat and dog, and I am horrified by the animal abuse in the news. Will these people who harm animals pay for it in the afterlife?

Answer: Our pets are beings with souls. They haven't reached the level of human evolution, but they are evolving as all life does in the Universe. All life on Earth has a consciousness. They have souls and oftentimes they return to be with us—reincarnation. Humans will be very surprised to find out where animals fit in in the spiritual realm. All that is done in the world is recorded on the Universal computer or Akashic Records, and many ignorant people think the harm they've done to animals will not count after they are dead. It will! All that the Creator has made is not to be taken lightly from the most lowly of life to the most magnificent. All life is precious and matters!!!

Humans kill all kinds of animals to eat. If we honored all life like the Indigenous people who take nothing for granted, our world would be in a better place. If we thanked the spirit that gave its life for us before eating it. Perhaps one-day humans will be more compassionate for the animals we eat. Did you know that animals taken to the slaughterhouses release the fear hormone before they died and then we eat that meat full of their fear hormone?

One day humans will exist on plant-based foods for all their needs.

Question: You posted an interview on Infowars.com with Alex Jones and Dr. Steve Pieczenik on November 11, 2020. What is the link to the show? They spoke about COVID and how Trump will be re-elected and could be in office for 8 years.

Answer: Dr. Steve Pieczenik discussed Trump's actions against the corrupt Deep State and the truth about COVID that he has witnessed as a doctor. Dr. Pieczenik is a Cuban-born American writer, publisher, psychiatrist, and a former United States Department of State official.
https://www.infowars.com/posts/trump-purging-deep-state-is-in-control-expert-reveals/

2021 Looking into The Future

CHAPTER SIXTEEN

THE MOON AND MARS

Question: I've read several of Michael Bara's books on Mars and the moon, and he has plenty of evidence that Martians once existed and a civilization on the moon. What do you see?

Answer: Scientists speculate that about 180 million years ago, a planet-shattering yet naturally occurring nuclear reaction may have wiped out everything on Mars, sending a shockwave that turned the planet into dry sand. Dr. John Brandenburg, a senior propulsion scientist at Orbital Technologies Corp. said, "The Martian surface is covered with a thin layer of radioactive substances including uranium, thorium and radioactive potassium—and this pattern radiates from a hot spot [on Mars]. A nuclear explosion could have sent debris all around the planet," he said. "Maps of gamma rays on Mars show a big red spot that seems like a radiating debris pattern—on the opposite side of the planet there is another red spot."

According to Brandenburg, the natural explosion, the equivalent of 1 million one-megaton hydrogen bombs, occurred in the northern Mare Acidalium region of Mars where there is a heavy concentration of radioactivity. "This explosion filled the Martian atmosphere with radioisotopes as well, which are seen in recent gamma-ray spectrometry data taken by NASA," he said. "The radioactivity also explains why the planet looks red."

If something so unimaginable could wipe out an entire civilization like Mars in the blink of an eye without anyone or any living creature surviving, could such a scenario happen to Earth?

I believe that many civilizations beyond our solar system have existed, some undeveloped and some highly advanced in sciences and technology. Some destroyed themselves, their environment through their foolish advances, and others were destroyed by enemies or asteroids. How can we believe that we are protected, and nothing will ever happen to Earth when the dinosaurs were wiped out instantly 65 million years ago?

The Moon

In the 1970s, before NASA began to erase moon photos taken by Apollo 8, 10, and 11, they published the NASA book sb2-46, showing a Moon city, a space base, tubes, roads, and vegetation. Also, the moon is supposed to have an atmosphere, 66% gravity compared to Earth's, and there is light, mining operations, and even a nuclear reactor there. Lear further claimed that to do this, extraterrestrial collaboration was necessary, and many buildings on the moon were already there before the operations began. this has been done over the past 50 years.

John's father had been involved with anti-gravity technology programs in the mid-1950s that is still secret technology today, according to a source known by John Lear within the U.S. government. Lear told Art Bell this:

- The population on Mars is around 600 million and the beings there are exactly like humans.
- He had worked with a part of the mining equipment that was to go to the Moon, he said: "We built this in Alabama, it was so big that when we finished the project, I took a small plane and flew over this piece of equipment to get an idea of how big it was."
- The most amazing thing is that there are many great authors, military or experts in espionage, space aeronautics, etc. that confirm many of these incredible statements made by Colonel Phil Corso,

Glen Steckling, Henry Deacon, Barr DiGregorio, and Gilbert Levin.

Strange petroglyphs exist in the southwest desert of what appears to be beings with antenna—the Ant people legend of the Hopi. Indigenous peoples have long held a belief in a subterranean world where the Ant beings inside the Earth helped them or saved their people. Gary A. David, the author of *Star Shrines and Earthworks of the Desert Southwest,* relates a most intriguing Hopi legend involving the Ant People, who were crucial to the survival of the Hopi—not just once but twice.

The so-called "First World" was apparently destroyed by fire or possibly some sort of volcanism, asteroid strike, or coronal mass ejection from the sun. The Second World was destroyed by ice—the Ice Age glaciers or a pole shift. During these two global cataclysms, the virtuous members of the Hopi tribe were guided by an odd-shaped cloud during the day and a moving star at night that led them to the sky god named *Sotuknang,* who finally took them to the Ant People—*Anu Sinom.* The Ant People then escorted the Hopi into subterranean caves where they found refuge and sustenance.

Another version of the myth is Spider Grandmother caused a hollow reed (or bamboo) to grow into the sky, and it emerged in the Fourth World at the *sipapu.* The people eventually climbed up a reed into this world, emerging from the *sipapu* from deep inside the Grand Canyon, an enchanted opening from the mysterious recesses of the Earth after a great flood which had drowned the previous third world.

The Hopi portrayed the Ant People as generous and industrious, giving the Hopi food when supplies ran short and teaching them the merits of food storage. Another legend states that the reason ants have such thin waists today is that they once deprived themselves of provisions to feed the Hopi. The Ant People were their saviors, taking them underground and teaching them how to survive two extreme cataclysms. The Sumerian texts and the Bible describe a horrific flood that covered the entire planet.

There's also a similarity to note with the Babylonian sky god who was named *Anu.* The Hopi word for "ant" is also *anu,* and the name for ant friends is *Anu Sinom*. It seems there is a direct link to the Anunnaki of the Sumerians. The Babylonian sky god was called *Anu,* which happens to be the Hopi word for ant. The word, *Naki* translates to "friends." Thus, *Anu-Naki* translates into "ant friend" in the Hopi language.

Another similar word is the Hopi word, *sohu*, which means "star", and the Egyptian word *sahu* means, "stars of Orion." The story of Orion and the Pleiades appear in the configuration of the pyramids of Egypt and other ancient structures.

When it was safe for the Hopi people to return to the surface, the Ant People instructed the building of incredibly complex habitations like that found at Chaco Canyon in northwestern New Mexico. From above, the structures look like a giant ant mound.

Today, the Ant People are honored by the Hopi with their headdresses and in their ceremonies. During religious ceremonies today, Hopi participants emerge from the kiva, a room or chamber built into the ground, from the plaza above, representing the original emergence by Puebloan people from the underground world to the current world.

The next story comes from SunBow's channeled book, *The Sasquatch Message to Humanity.* Keep in mind the prior information on the Hopi legends of the Ant People. He says the Ant People eventually moved to the first moon to colonize it. They began leaving their underwater and underground bases in silvery disks. The lower lords started chasing and shooting down their flying craft, bringing the war of hybrids out of the underworld into the skies. This caused great destruction and death on our planet, causing the Star Elders to intervene. They could not allow the destruction of Earth and Soul evolution.

It soon became obvious that the Moon could not sustain the growing Ant People population of biological clones. They began to dig deep into the moon to hollow it out and used the silicon-based dust to create synthetic clones. The biological Ant People remained within the Earth underground while the clones grew larger.

The Reptilians began to use a new weapon of mass destruction to destroy the cloned Ant People. (It's more involved than this, but this is the shortened version of a long story.) The new activities caught the attention of the lower lords in the underworld, who had further planned to destroy the Ant People. These lower lords launched massive nuclear strikes on the hollowed moon, causing its thin shell to collapse and the natural satellite that Earth had provided to implode and be turned into a cloud of debris. This destruction of the Moon caused the fourth mass extinction event on Earth. Only a few of the Ant People were able to fly off the Moon before the implosion.

For ages, the surface of the Earth was darkened by clouds of dust and debris from meteors that rained down from the sky. This caused another step in the evolution of certain species to develop wings and later fly. Their scales turned to feathers through genetic mutation.

The next plan was to create an artificial Moon, to replace the natural one where the Ant People had evolved. Earth's gravitational field had increased since the destruction of the natural Moon, pulling the thickened atmosphere into denser, heavier substances. With a new moon, Earth's atmosphere would improve conditions for biological life, producing a higher, thinner atmosphere, and speeding up the Earth's rotation and life cycles. For these reasons, the Star Elders allowed the Ant People to build a new Moon, for the continuity of their evolutionary process.

This construction of the new artificial Moon took thousands of years to build by the arms of synthetic Ant People. That is why sharp edges, geometric structures, and signs of engineering are seen on the Moon's surface. Who knows, perhaps there is great truth in this story, especially when you consider this—between 1972 and 1977, NASA installed seismometers on the Moon on Apollo missions and recorded moonquakes. The Moon was described as "ringing like a bell" during some of those quakes, specifically the shallow ones. When Apollo 12 deliberately crashed the Ascent Stage of its Lunar Module onto the Moon's surface, NASA claimed that the Moon rang like a bell for an hour, leading to theories by conspiracy theorists that the Moon was hollow and perhaps an artificial satellite. Vast chambers beneath the Moon perhaps caused the Moon to ring like a bell.

The condition given to the Ant People by the Star Elders Council for its construction was that they would never again create an invasive species, nor plan another invasion anywhere on Earth.

The Star Elders offered protection to the Ant People as long as they upheld this covenant.

The Ant People survived three mass extinction events and each time a near disappearance of their lineage. From this, they learned about the fragility of life. They also learned that overpopulating their environment caused a threat to themselves, so they slowed down their reproduction rate. This is a powerful lesson that should be learned by the current inhabitants of the Earth!

According to SunBow's channeled information, the types of life forms inhabiting the whole Omniverse is beyond our comprehension. It is impossible to know or to describe all forms of life and it would not be necessary or useful. All those infinitely diversified life forms serve but one purpose—the evolution of Soul consciousness! When the individual souls' emotional experience reaches empathy and compassion, their consciousness starts to understand intelligence and the spiritual meaning of life. As they rise into higher levels of consciousness, compassionate souls are guided to use their incarnations for spiritual evolution. Along the path, they eventually learn that spiritual consciousness rises through healing karmic debts.

Pharaoh Sety describes a Distant World Cataclysm

This bizarre story is probably too incredible to be believed, but the details in the description are too eerie to discount. Perhaps the description is Mars where an unknown cataclysmic event killed everyone and all the creatures instantly where they stood. The story is told in the book, *The Search for Omm Sety,* by Jonathan Cott, published in 1987, about the true story of Dorothy Eady, born in England in 1904. At the age of three, Dorothy fell down a flight of stairs and was pronounced dead by Eady's family doctor. Hours later after preparing her body for burial, she awakened as if nothing happened, but Dorothy was changed.

Dorothy began insisting that her parents were not her true parents. After her father had brought home an encyclopedia, the little girl was found reading stories of Egypt and was fascinated with the ancient country. Dorothy began to dream of Egypt with its columns and beautiful gardens and trees. The first time Dorothy was taken to the British Museum in London, she rushed to the

Egyptian exhibit and found the mummy of Pharaoh Sety I, refusing to leave. There was something familiar about Sety that she didn't understand.

Through the years the apparition of Sety I began to appear to her. As an adult, Dorothy eventually married an Egyptian man and moved to Cairo where she worked for the Department of Antiquities in deciphering hieroglyphs. It was during this time that the ghost of Pharaoh Sety appeared to her often and was even witnessed by friends and family. He told her of their love, and they became lovers during his reign when she was a High Priestess. After learning she was pregnant with Sety's child, she committed suicide. After his death, Sety searched for her throughout the cosmos and finally found her reincarnated as Dorothy Eady. Year later, Dorothy Eady became known in Egypt as Omm Sety, *"Mother of Seti."*

Dorothy made this entry in her journal about Sety's visit on August 29, 1974, after he had been absent for 20 days. He told her a story that was both strange and frightening. He told her how maddened he was with sorrow thinking he would never find his beloved.

He said, "I began a search—I reached the skies, and in so doing I found that some, and therefore perhaps all, of the stars were worlds. But they were strange and hateful. Now, Little One (referring to Dorothy), I will tell you the most horrible thing. I found a world on which people had lived. There were great cities with very tall buildings built of large blocks of red stone that had glittering particles in it.

(Sety might have described the red planet Mars due to deposits of iron rusting on the planet's surface. Rocks and soil on the surface of Mars contain dust composed mostly of iron and small amounts of other elements such as chlorine and sulfur).

"There were fine, wide streets, and some of them had part of the way paved with shining metal of bright blue. In fact, in the very place where we would have used copper, there was this beautiful blue metal. In the streets lay long metal things with windows and seats inside, but they had neither wings like the metal birds nor wheels. Inside there were people, like us, but much taller, and they were all dead. In the tall houses, in the streets, in the workshops (which had many strange things made of blue metal) were many people, men and women, and children, and all were dead. They were not decayed; their flesh had dried like that of a *sahu* (incorruptible soul). But none of them had any hair on their heads or bodies, or on their faces. I saw a large, open space like those where the metal birds alight, and there were many of those strange metal things; some of which were full of dead people, some empty, some had people inside, and others about to enter, when they all died.

"One lay at a distance. It was broken, and most of the people in it were broken. They all seem to have died suddenly; each one in his place. Most of them had a look of horror on their faces. It was terrible to behold. Also, I think that they were people of high culture, and they seem to have had many things that the people of the Earth use today. In some houses, I saw pictures made of light. The clothes of the people were strange. They were all alike—men and women, long coverings for the legs and short tunics, and they were made of a strange material that was not woven, but was like papyrus, but seemingly soft and pliable.

"A terrible thing about the place is that there was no air, not a faint breeze stirred. There was no water. Outside the city were vast fields of cultivated plants, all standing dry and motionless, and tall trees, dead and dry, and not a breeze to blow their dry leaves away. There were also some strange looking animals, all dead, and one still had a mouthful of plants partly in its mouth. I was horrified and sick at heart, and I fled back to *Amenti* (Sety's afterlife world)."

Dorothy had many detailed conversations with Sety on ancient Egypt, Atlantis, and the Pharaoh Akhenaton. The description by Sety during his astral travels to find Dorothy on this distant world were too detailed. Perhaps Sety was describing Mars or far distance world in our solar system, but whatever caused their demise, natural or unnatural, happened instantly before the beings of this world could escape. Could this explain why many NASA photographs appear to man-made objects on the surface of Mars, i.e. the Face of Mars, pyramid shapes, miles of glass tubes, that might have been created by technologically advanced beings? The problem appears to be NASA's ability to erase or cover-up photographs of objects captured on Mars and then tell us that they are natural formations. So why the big secret and coverup?

Author Mike Bara in his book, *Ancient Aliens on Mars,* provided plenty of NASA photographs of objects and oddities that can be explained away as natural. Of course, debunkers and skeptical panned the book, but as I say, "If it walks like a duck and quacks like a duck, it's probably a duck." In other words, Occam's Razor—the simplest answer is always the best one."

According to NASA's Curiosity Rover, Mars at times can become windy with speeds up to 62 mph. For the first time, NASA scientists have found a large, watery lake beneath an ice cap on Mars. Because water is essential to life, the discovery offers an exciting new place to search for life-forms beyond Earth. There is not much air on Mars—the atmospheric pressure there is less than one one-hundredth of what we breathe on Earth but what little is there has baffled planetary scientists.

Author's Remote Viewing of Mars

In 1976 I dreamed or remotely viewed a group of scientists at JPL (Jet Propulsion Laboratory in Pasadena, California) viewing a large screen on the wall. What caught my attention was the screen and a desert-like scene reminiscent of the Southwest desert of the United States. The screen moved and there were huge pyramid structures and then what looked like a huge landing ramp and giant formations in the ground. I heard one scientist say, "Mars!" excitedly. The men patted one another on the back and others shook hands as if congratulating each other on the discovery they were viewing on the screen.

Through the years I have experienced clairvoyant dreams of the future, but never what I would call "remote viewing" where I was watching something happen in real-time in my astral body.

In the 1980s, I was invited to a dinner party by a married couple in Los Angeles, known for the artwork. They had invited a NASA computer scientist named Frank. During dinner, I sat beside Frank and decided to quiz him about my remote viewing of Mars at JPL and asked if pyramid structures, a huge landing ramp and circular formations in the ground had been photograph by NASA.

Frank stared at me for several minutes, and finally said, "How do you know about those classified photographs?" I was shocked by his answer and explained how I was at JPL watching a large screen. He then said, choosing his word carefully, "The Viking mission to Mars in 1976 photographed structures that looked man-made." He didn't elaborate because the information was top-secret, but he said that was I did see at JPL was mostly accurate.

One year later, I asked my friends about Frank, and they had not seen or heard from him since the dinner party.

Recently in a series of tweets, Elon Musk revealed new details about his plan to build a city of 1 million people on Mars by 2050. Musk said he hoped to build 1,000 Starships — the towering and ostensibly fully reusable spaceship that SpaceX is developing in South Texas—over 10 years. Trump wants his Space Force and Elon Musk want to put 1 million people on Mars by 2050. Musk is aiming for Mars cargo missions by 2022 and a manned Mars mission by 2024. Eventually, the goal would be to launch 1,000 Starship flights to Mars every year – an average of three per day. Each trip would see 100 passengers make their way to the Red Planet to become citizens of a Mars megacity. Based on Musk's projections, it would take a fleet of 1,000 Starships around nine years to carry a million people to Mars.

During an interview on Art Bell's Coast to Coast talk show, John Lear revealed that humans have been secretly visiting the moon since 1962, and also humans have been on Mars since 1966. He claimed that NASA used technology from alien spacecraft crashed on earth in 1953.

During the 1970s, before NASA began to erase moon photos taken by Apollo 8, 10, and 11, they published the NASA book sb2-46, showing a moon city, a space base, tubes, roads, and vegetation. also, the moon is supposed to have an atmosphere, 66% gravity compared to earth's, and there is light, mining operations, and even a nuclear reactor there. Lear further claimed that to do this, extraterrestrial collaboration was necessary, and many buildings on the moon were already there before the operations began. this has been done over the past 50 years.

2021 Looking into The Future

CHAPTER SEVENTEEN

THEORIES ON COVID

Did the Chinese mastermind the Coronavirus in their laboratories and did it accidentally escape? The virus was well planned and ready to be released on the world. Was it a way to cull the herd of Earth's 7.8 billion people? Although we are told that over 1 million people have died from COVID-19, I believe that China lied about the deaths in their country, and North Korea claims they have no COVID cases.

On October 1, 2020, Trump announced to the world that he and First Lady Melania have been infected with COVID-19. Trump was admitted to Walter Reed National Military Medical Center and received a cocktail of Remdesivir and Regeneron, both controversial antiviral medications never combined before. Trump made a speedy recovery and went back to campaigning.

Shortly before Trump was admitted, an event in the Rose Garden of the White House was held to announce President Trump's nomination of Judge Amy Coney Barrett to the Supreme Court. Numerous people attending became infected. Again, Biden berated Trump for inviting all these people, and most of them didn't wear masks, but that wasn't Trump's fault. These were adults who knew better. Former White House counselor Kellyanne Conway, Republican Sen. Ron Johnson of Wisconsin, Trump's campaign manager Bill Stepien, Former Governor of New Jersey Chris Christy, Senator Mike Lee, Trump's aide Hope Hicks, White House secretary Kayleigh McEnany, Trump's son Barron Trump and the First Lady Melania all tested positive for Coronavirus. And thankfully, all have survived.

How this virus traveled around the globe in such a short time? Of course, people travel every day worldwide, but even after the shutdown, the virus spread a warped speed. Viruses circulate Earth's atmosphere and fall from it, according to new research from scientists in Canada, Spain, and the United States. The study marks the first-time scientists have quantified the viruses being swept up from Earth's surface into the free troposphere, beyond Earth's weather systems but below the stratosphere where jet airplanes fly. The viruses can be carried thousands of kilometers before being deposited back onto the Earth's surface.

"Every day, more than 800 million viruses are deposited per square meter above the planetary boundary layer—that's 25 viruses for each person in Canada. Roughly 20 years ago we began finding genetically similar viruses occurring in very different environments around the globe," said the University of British Columbia virologist Curtis Suttle, one of the senior authors of a paper in the International Society for Microbial Ecology Journal that outlines the findings. "This preponderance of long-residence viruses traveling the atmosphere likely explains why—it's quite conceivable to have a virus swept up into the atmosphere on one continent and deposited on another."

If this study is true, that gives greater credence to the chemtrail spraying worldwide. According to those who have researched chemtrails for years like Dane Wigington, (not contrails that are water vapor) chemtrails contain aluminum and barium, which can affect the human biosystem, cause autism in children, cancers, Alzheimer's Disease, and other dire health issues and has also caused the great wildfires worldwide. It's called geoengineering of Earth's weather—it's weather warfare by the Family of Dark.

Aluminum sucks the moisture from crops, plants and forests. The tree becomes saturated with aluminum particulates that enter into the root, and the plant or tree begins to die and can't fight off disease or insects such as the beetles that have killed thousands of trees. Aluminum also removed all the moisture in the atmosphere.

Since the late 1990s, I have observed these unnatural clouds called "chemtrails" laid down by unmarked jets covering skies throughout the United States and observed throughout the world. I'd observe a clear morning sky, and by early afternoon the sky was covered in crisscrossed trails that spread across the entire sky. Often, the chemtrails are sprayed from the mysterious white unmarked jets before a weather front was forecast to move in the Northwest. What should have brought rain never materialized. This has been going on for years.

People refuse to believe this is happening because of the fake news and social media debunking. As a child I watched jets fly over and see the condensation behind it, which vanishes within minutes. It never spread across the sky. When humans are bombarded with fake news, they believe it. We are easily mind-controlled. The truth is our weather and climate have been altered by chemtrails (nano-materials) and it's going to get worse, my friends. Isn't it odd that when the shutdown took place the chemtrails vanished for a few weeks?

Our precious planet is dying!

If you don't believe that the Family of Dark is trying to destroy us and this planet, think again! Our governments have been conducting experiments on unsuspecting civilians for years. The U.S. military carried out atomic/nuclear tests above and below ground for years. People in the surrounding towns of the Southwest have developed horrible cancers from the radiation fallout.

In 1950, the U.S. Navy sprayed a cloud of bacteria from ships over San Francisco, California to find out how susceptible an American City would be to a biological attack. A large number of people became ill with pneumonia-like symptoms. During Gulf War's Desert Storm Operation, 1990-1991, soldiers complained of mysterious chronic symptoms known as the Gulf War syndrome, but the military denied their illnesses ever existed. Approximately 250,000 to 697,000 U.S. veterans who served in the 1991 Gulf War were afflicted with chronic multi-symptom illness, a condition with serious consequences. What they suffered from was determined to be biological nerve agents, germ warfare like sarin gas, cyclosarin, and emissions from oil well fires.

Between 1929 and 1974, it is estimated that 65,000 people were victims of forced sterilization in at least 30 states, and nearly 7,600 people were sterilized under the orders from North Carolina's Eugenics Board. From 1950 to 1973, Project MKUltra mind-control program was put into place by the CIA. Experiments on humans were intended to identify and develop drugs and procedures to be used in interrogations to weaken the individual and force confessions through mind-control. Both children and adults were used unknowingly for these experiments. Other military and CIA projects included Project Bluebird and Project Artichoke and coordinated with the United States Army Biological Warfare Laboratories.

Another insane study conducted by United States Public Health Service from 1932 to 1972 involved African American men receiving syphilis, known as the Tuskegee Syphilis Study or Experiment. The men were only told they were receiving free health care from the Federal government of the United States.

Many evil people exist in our world who care nothing about you or me. What is their motive? To destroy us and take over the world. While the Earth is being destroyed, they will go deep into their underground bunkers that are equipped with everything. These bunkers are rumored to be as big as cities where tunnels go for miles across the United States. The tunnels carry people by bullet trains.

Wildfires in 2020 and into 2021

Like 2020, I foresee horrible wildfires. This winter/spring 2020 will see rains and mudslides in areas ravaged by wildfires. More death and destruction.

In the past few years, wildfires have consumed millions of acres of land in Siberia, the rainforests of Brazil, Australia, and the United States. In January 2020, Australian wildfires were declared among the 'worst wildlife disasters in modern history.' More than 46 million acres were scorched and along with the plant life, an estimated 1.25 billion animals were killed or injured.

In 2019, record-breaking fires ripped through the rainforests of the Amazon—an ecosystem on which the entire planet depends on.

California Department of Forestry and Fire Protection (CAL FIRE) said they have never seen fires burn as hot as the fires of 2020 in Northern and Southern California. Even fire tornadoes were seen. Wildfires have burned an unprecedented swath of California this year, scorching nearly 4 million acres — an area larger than Connecticut — and killing 31 people, according to the California Department of Forestry and Fire Protection. A number of the fires were set by arsonists. Previously, California's worst year of fire was in 2018, when more than 1.8 million acres were burned and more than 100 people were killed, according to the National Interagency Coordination Center.

Fires in 2020 have destroyed more than 8,200 structures and, as of Friday, had displaced more than 53,000 from their homes. The property damage toll has not yet approached that of 2018 when more than 17,000 homes and 700 businesses were destroyed. Lightning in August ignited many of California's biggest blazes, but scientists say climate change has also contributed to the conflagrations. It was the hottest August on record in California and the entire Southwest. Trees and brush were already abnormally dry and combustible after northern and central California saw exceptionally dry conditions last winter.

In 2015, Prince Ea, a 31-year-old activist, hip-hop artist, and filmmaker, produced a YouTube video titled, *Dear Future Generations: Sorry*. In the video, he says: "Sorry that we were too caught up in our doings to do something. Sorry that we listened to people who made excuses to do nothing. I hope you forgive us, but we just didn't realize how special the Earth was. We didn't know what we had until it was gone. You probably know it as the Amazon desert now but believe it or not, it was once called the Amazon Rainforest and there were billions of trees. They were gorgeous. You don't know much about trees, do you?

"Trees are amazing. We literally breathe the air they are creating. THEY CLEAN UP OUR POLLUTION AND CARBON. They store and purify our water and give us medicine for diseases, give us food to feed us and that is why I am so sorry to tell you we burned them down, cut them with brutal machines, horrific at 40 football fields a minute. That is 50 percent of all trees gone in the last 100 years.

"Sorry that we left you with a mess of a planet. When I was a child, I read how the Native Americans had such consideration for the planet for how they left the land for the next seven generations. This brings me great sorrow because most of us today don't care about tomorrow. I'm sorry that we put profit above people, greed above need, and the rule of gold above the golden rule. I am sorry that we used nature as a credit card with no spending limit, over-drafting animals to extinction before we could become friends with them. Sorry, we poisoned the oceans, so much you can't swim in them, but most of all I'm sorry about our mindset cause we have the nerve to call this destruction...PROGRESS."

Trees are dying worldwide from what scientists say is from "Climate Change." Most are afraid to use climate change or warming. Many of California's other tree species are already known to be at risk. The record-breaking drought that plagued the state from 2011-2016 killed an estimated 129 million trees, mostly in the state's mixed-conifer forests that include trees like white fir, only exist in California and they require 1000 gallons of water daily to survive.

From 2018 article: While researching for his new novel, author Denis Mills discovered an alarming link between chemtrails and the super wildfires. The author discovered that unprecedented levels of aluminum and barium nanodust, primary components in chemtrails, both of which are incendiary, are fueling the ferocity of the super wildfires.

A retired USAF brigadier general, Gen. Charles Jones, has been quoted from a public source as stating, "These white aircraft spray trails are the result of scientifically verifiable spraying of aluminum particles and other toxic heavy metals, polymers and chemicals. Millions of tons of aluminum and barium are being sprayed almost daily across the U.S., stated Mills, a former naval officer, and UCLA graduate. "Just sprinkle aluminum or barium dust on a fire and see what happens. It's near explosive. When wildfires break out, the aluminum/barium dust results in levels of fire intensity so great as to cause firefighters to coin a new term, 'firenado,' " he said. The entire U.S., in addition to various other NATO countries, are being sprayed."

The government has for years denied the existence of chemtrail spraying. It now calls the program by various names, all under Geoengineering.

According to Cal Fire operation chief Steve Crawford, the fires are burning differently and more aggressively. It has been reported the fires move faster than anyone has ever seen and barriers that in years past contained them such as rivers, no longer do.

In California's Mt. Shasta region, Francis Mangel, a USDA biologist tested and found elevated levels of aluminum in water and soil samples of 4,610 parts per million which are 25,000 times the safe guidelines of the World Health Organization. No one can argue, however, the wildfires' newfound ferocity or the millions of tons of aluminum/barium nanodust which have appeared, which is killing vegetation and causing illness and death.

2021 Looking into The Future

CHAPTER EIGHTEEN

UFOs OVER NUCLEAR FACILITIES

Thirteen years ago, only a select few people knew that the U.S. Congress authorized a secret study of UFOs and nuclear weapon facilities. In 2007, Senate majority leader Harry Reid and two of his most trusted Senate colleagues conferred in a highly secure room about the perplexing mystery of UFOs. The three senators agreed to authorize black budget funds for a study by the Defense Intelligence Agency (DIA) into UFO incidents and related phenomena.

In 1955, 14 A-bombs were detonated as part of Operation Teapot at the Nevada test site, witnessed by thousands of military personnel in trenches, and by thousands of test site employees. But there were other observers as well. "It was what we called flying saucers. They were pretty prevalent at the test site back then," said a former test site photographer.

At least a dozen former test site employees have told similar stories about unknown aircraft showing up hours or days after an atomic blast.

In addition to the eyewitness accounts, thousands of pages of formerly classified documents have been released. A Freedom of Information Act request filed in 1992 produced a large stack of documents from the Department of Energy (DOE), indicating UFO incidents over every major atomic weapons facility dating back to the late 1940s, over Los Alamos National Lab, where the bombs were designed, and over Hanford, where the plutonium was processed. But DOE has no records of any official sightings over what later became the Nevada Test Site. However, plenty was found.

The government ended atomic weapons tests years ago, but

Nevada incidents continue. Former security officers at Area 2 at Nellis Air Force Base, for years a storage facility for up to 200 nuclear warheads, have reported multiple intrusions by unknown aircraft from the late 1990s through 2004.

Several military officers have come forward with cases in which UFOs have interfered and deactivated nuclear weapons and installations. One of these officers is Dr. Robert Jacobs who in 1965 was stationed at the Vandenberg air-force base in California. Jacobs came forward with his story in 1982 and has in recent years been interviewed several times.

Back in 1965, Jacobs was stationed at the Vandenberg base and in charge of all photo and optical equipment. His team had installed a camera on a telescope on a nearby mountain which was used to film the launch and trajectory of intercontinental ballistic missiles. The test launches served to ensure readiness for a nuclear attack on the Soviet Union. The engineering team would install dummy nuclear warheads of the same size, dimension, and weight as the real ones and launch. Since most missiles failed engineering teams required footage of the missiles´ trajectory and behavior to review and identify possible causes of failure.

On January 8, 1965, an Atlas F-missile was launched from the base. The missile took off and everything indicated that the filming was executed perfectly. Jacobs and his team were happy that everything seemed to have worked according to plan. The team was too busy celebrating that nobody looked through the telescope to take a close look at the missile's flight path. All they could see with the naked eye was a smoke trail. However, at an altitude of about 60 miles, something unimaginable was unfolding. A few moments later they heard the camera´s film wrap off (the cameras back then were not digital). They took the film off the camera and dispatched it to the base.

One or two days later, Jacobs was called into Major Florenz J. Mannsman's office, his superior. Walking into the office, Jacobs saw a screen and a projector set-up and two individuals in gray suits. The major introduced them to Jacobs by just giving their first names and saying that they had come from Washington D.C. Jacobs was then asked to sit on the couch as the major turned on the projector and played the recording from the recent launch.

They watched the three burnouts (i.e. missiles are launched with a series of rocket systems, once one runs out of fuel it is dropped and the next rocket takes over), after a few moments the major said, "Watch this a bit closely." Suddenly they see a disc-shaped UFO enter the film frame flying next to the missile. Then, the UFO emitted a beam of light to the missile's warhead (dummy nuclear warhead for a test launch). It changed its position and moved over the missile and emitted a second beam. The UFO repeated the same action two more times from different angles and flew away from the scene.

A few seconds later, the missile tumbled out of control never making it to its intended target. The major turned on the light and asked for explanations. Jacobs could only explain this intervention as a UFO. Next, Major Mannsman smiled and said, "You are not to say anything about this footage, as far as you and I are concerned it never happened! Right?" Jacobs agreed and the film was handed over to the two men in gray suits. At the end of the meeting, Jacobs was also warned of the consequences of coming forward with the story.

Jacobs kept silent for 17 years but realized that he could speak about this specific incident because nobody had formally told him it was classified as top secret. After these revelations, Jacobs was harassed at work and received many threats mostly over the telephone. This case is one of a series of testimonies indicating that unknown alien civilizations are concerned about our use of nuclear weapons and have the capabilities to deter us.

One of the more out-of-the-ordinary press conferences was held in Washington in the month of September in 2010 and consisted of former Air Force personnel testifying to the existence of UFOs and their ability to neutralize American and Russian nuclear missiles.

UFO researcher Robert Hastings of Albuquerque, N.M., who organized the National Press Club briefing, said more than 120 former service members had told him they'd seen unidentified flying objects near nuclear weapon storage and testing grounds.

Air Force Capt. Robert Salas, who was at Malmstrom Air Force Base in Montana in 1967 when 10 ICMs he was overseeing suddenly became inoperative - at the same time base security informed him of a mysterious red glowing object in the sky.

Robert Jamison, a retired USAF nuclear missile targeting officer, told of several occasions having to go out and "re-start" missiles that had been deactivated after UFOs were sighted nearby. Similar sightings at nuclear sites in the former Soviet Union and Britain were related.

CBS Affiliate KSWT described "Britain's Roswell," a case of unidentified phenomena in December 1980 incident near two Royal Air Force Bases in Suffolk, England. Several U.S. Air Force personnel reported seeing a strange metallic object hovering in Rendlesham Forest near RAF Woodbridge and found three depressions in the ground.

Retired USAF Col. Charles Halt said that in December 1980, when he was deputy base commander at RAF (Royal Air Force) Bentwaters, strange lights in the forest were investigated by three patrolmen. Halt said they reported approaching a triangular craft, "approximately three meters on a side, dark metallic in appearance with strange markings. They were observing it for a period of time, and then it very quickly and silently vanished at high speed."

Two nights later, Halt investigated another sighting near the base when he was told by the base commander, "It's back." Halt found indentations in the ground, broken branches, and low-level background radiation. He and his team also witnessed various lights moving silently in the sky, of one which was "shedding something like molten metal." Another shined a beam of light down towards them.

The incidents were never officially explained.

Several of the ex-service members speaking said that when they had brought their concern of such appearances to superiors, they'd been told it was "top secret" or that it "didn't happen."

Hastings suggested the presence of such phenomena meant that aliens were monitoring our weapons, and perhaps warning us—"a sign to Washington and Moscow that we are playing with fire, as quoted in the Telegraph.

Hastings predicted a "paradigm shift" in the mindset of humanity to the existence of alien life. "Traditional institutions such as religions, governments, other social institutions may be threatened by what is coming. That is just the logical consequence of what is about to occur."

The U.S. Air Force ended its 22-year-long Project Blue Book investigation of UFO sightings after investigating 12,618 sightings; all but 701 were explained, and the reminder was categorized as "unidentified" due to sketchy reports, a Pentagon spokesman said in 1997. "We cannot substantiate the existence of UFOs, and we are not harboring the remains of UFOs," said Pentagon spokesperson Kenneth Bacon in 1997. "I can't be more clear about it than that."

Aliens came to Earth to stop a nuclear war between America and Russia, according to the bizarre claim of former astronaut Edgar Mitchell (1930-2016), the sixth man to walk on the moon. He claimed that high-ranking military officials witnessed alien ships during weapons tests throughout the 1940s.

The UFOs, he said, were spotted hovering over the world's first nuclear weapons test which took place on July 16, 1945, in the desolate White Sands deserts of New Mexico.

The NSA veteran had regularly spoken about his belief in aliens since he landed on the surface of the moon during the Apollo 14 mission in 1971. Mitchell said, "They wanted to know about our military capabilities. My own experience talking to people has made it clear the ETs had been attempting to keep us from going to war and help create peace on Earth."

Mitchell claimed that stories from people who manned missile bases during the 20th century back up his claims. "Other officers from bases on the Pacific coast told me their [test] missiles were frequently shot down by alien spacecraft," he said.

He previously said supposedly real-life ET's were similar to the traditional image of a small frame, large eyes, and head. He claimed our technology is 'not nearly as sophisticated' as theirs and 'had they been hostile', he warned 'we would be been gone by now.'

Nick Pope, a former Ministry of Defense UFO researcher, told DailyMail.com that Dr. Mitchell's comments are all based on second-hand reports. "Even where Mitchell's sources are genuine, how do we know they have access to classified information about UFOs?" questioned Pope.

Conspiracy theorists say it is no coincidence that aliens showed up very shortly after we had developed atomic weapons and rocket technology, as this is when they were alerted to the threat we pose to the wider cosmos. "Ironically, governments have sometimes secretly promoted belief in UFOs, because if someone sees a secret prototype aircraft or drone, it's much better to have it reported as a flying saucer than recognized for what it is," said Pope. "None of this is to say that there haven't been some genuinely fascinating and unexplained UFO sightings around nuclear facilities and military bases, but just because a UFO sighting is unexplained, it doesn't follow that it's extraterrestrial. In a final irony, the very conspiracy theorists who believe Edgar Mitchell when he talks about aliens don't believe him when he talks about his moon mission, because they think it was all done on a film set."

Dr. Mitchell, who had a Bachelor of Science degree in aeronautical engineering and a Doctor of Science degree in Aeronautics and Astronautics, also said the Roswell cover-up was real. "This is really starting to open up,' he told a radio show several years ago. "I think we're headed for real disclosure and some serious organizations are moving in that direction."

Officials from NASA were quick to downplay the comments. In a statement at the time, a spokesman said: "NASA does not track UFOs. NASA is not involved in any sort of cover-up about alien life on this planet or anywhere in the universe. Dr. Mitchell is a great American, but we do not share his opinions on this issue."

While Edgar Mitchell believed aliens attempted to save Earth from nuclear war, others have claimed ET proved it. But if the aliens were so concerned about our nuclear abilities, why didn't they stop the U.S. from dropping two nuclear bombs on Hiroshima and Nagasaki, Japan on August 6 and 9, 1945 that killed an estimated 226,900 people, mostly citizens?

CHAPTER NINETEEN

THE RETURN OF JESUS

Religions all over the world have awaited the return of Jesus or the Christ to return in physical form and save us. If such an evolved teacher, and there have been many that have walked the Earth, returned, but would we realize such a Master?

Most likely if Jesus returned, had healing powers, and taught ancient wisdom, he would be branded the antichrist or a demon, or even a cult leader. He would be denied as he was over 2,000 years ago. Why would such a spiritually evolved soul really want to return at this time when humans show little compassion for others or interest in higher spiritual learning?

In the book, *The Watchers*, by Raymond Fowler, abductee Betty Andreasson Luca, a very spiritual woman, was told by the tall human-looking Elder that they loved Jesus and that he would be coming back soon, perhaps for Betty's benefit to keep her calm.

During one of many of Betty's fantastical experiences in 1967, she was shown a dazzling bright light in front of an enormous bird. As she approached the bird, the temperature became unbearably hot, and Betty nearly fainted from the intensity of it. When she opened her eyes, the light was dimmed, and the bird had vanished. All she saw was a small fire that slowly turned to ashes, out of which, emerged a gray worm, like the mythical legend of the Phoenix bird where it consumes itself and is reborn again from the ashes, symbolic of reincarnation.

I have received emails from people asking if Jesus will return? I don't feel a physical return will happen in our lifetimes, but I do feel his presence in the spiritual realm as he walks among us.

During the 1980s, people believe Jesus had returned as Maitreya, the World Teacher, and was living in London at the time, according to Scottish artist, author, and esotericist, Benjamin Crème (1922-2016). This was the second coming prophesied by many religions.

At that time, I worked for the Disney Studios in Burbank, California where several coworkers believed in Maitreya and wanted me to get involved with the new age movement. On May 14, 1982, Benjamin Crème held a press conference in Los Angeles. More than 90 reporters attended and heard Crème announce that Maitreya was living in the Asian community in the Brick Lane area of London, England. Crème also presented a challenge to the reports that if they made a serious attempt to seek Maitreya in London, he would reveal himself to them.

By the spring of 1982, Crème placed advertisements in newspapers around the world stating, "The Christ is now here." According to Crème, the Christ, who he called Maitreya, would announce his existence on worldwide television broadcasts. Maitreya's face would appear simultaneously on every screen on the globe and communicate telepathically to everyone: "his thoughts, his ideas, his call to humanity for justice, sharing, right relationships, and peace, will take place silently, telepathically. Each of us will hear him inwardly in our own language."

Crème further stated in newspaper advertisements that the Second Coming of Christ would occur on Monday, June 21, 1982, during the summer solstice.

Skeptical, I knew the announcement would never happen. After 1982, Crème made several additional predictions and announcements about the imminent appearance of Maitreya, based on his claims of receiving telepathic messages from the Master of Wisdom. In January 1986, Maitreya contacted media representatives at the highest level in Britain who agreed to make an announcement. Under pressure from high religious and government officials, however, this statement was withheld.

Crème also claimed that "On February 26, 1987, Maitreya gave an interview to the major American television company, Cable News Network (CNN). He was interviewed under His ordinary, everyday name, and did not call Himself the Christ. He did say, however, that, among other names, He was known as Maitreya. A group of His closest associates journeyed to the United States to arrange further interviews. The CNN interview was made available for possible showing in 26 of a promised 29 countries in Europe, Scandinavia, North Africa, and the Middle East, but was not broadcast in the United States. The CNN office in Atlanta explained that they could not see a framework in which to present the interview.

Crème also claimed he was first contacted telepathically by his Master in January 1959, when he was asked to make tape recordings of his messages.

Maitreya's message announced the emergence of a group of enlightened spiritual teachers who would guide humanity forward into the new Aquarian Age of peace and brotherhood based on principles of love and sharing. At the head of this group would be a great Avatar, Maitreya, the World Teacher, expected by all the major religions as their "Awaited One"—the Christ to the Christians, the Iman Madhi to the Muslims, the Messiah for the Jews, and the 5th Buddha (Maitreya) for the Buddhists.

During an interview in 2006, Creme confirmed his views on the importance of Crop Circles: "The UFOs have an enormous part to play in the security of this planet at the ecological level. [The crop circles are part of] a new science that will give us energy directly from the sun. Oil will become a thing of the past. No one will be able to sell energy in the future."

In Theosophical texts, Maitreya is said to have had numerous manifestations or incarnations: in the theorized ancient continent of Atlantis; as a Hierophant in Ancient Egypt; as the Hindu deity Krishna; as a high priest in Ancient India; and as Christ during the three years of the Ministry of Jesus.

The Maitreya that Benjamin Creme spoke of, and who spoke through Creme via a process called "over-shadowing", was one of a secret brotherhood of Ascended Masters who have been guiding humanity for millennia and more. He left his Himalayan sanctuary in the late 1970s having been roused by starvation and the suffering of innocent children to teach the world universal brotherhood.

Two thousand years before, he had "manifested" through his disciple Jesus, and now he felt the 20th century needed him. He grew himself a suitable body and boarded a jumbo jet from Pakistan to Heathrow. From there he headed to Brick Lane to merge with the Bangladeshi community and take a job as a night porter at a hospital. He telepathically communicated with Creme, teleported to the shrines of the faithful, and made signs for believers to share with the world: lights in the sky, handprints left on windows, a visitation here or there. His arrival was heralded by small and diverse miracles.

Was Maitreya a hoax by Crème or was there a master who walked among us and no one recognized him?

Maitreya walking among the people of Nairobi, Kenya
Year unknown

Perhaps I should let you all in on a little secret. No one likes you in the future. This time is looked at as being full of lazy, self-centered, civically ignorant sheep. —Time Traveler John Titor

CHAPTER TWENTY

THE COMING CIVIL WAR

Numerous people have written and asked if I foresee another civil war in the United States. I hate to be the bearer of bad news, but a civil war is coming to America and it's been building for many years. The trigger will be the outcome of the election and it doesn't matter who is elected as President, the fight will begin. Already Antifa members are conducting occult rituals in the streets of Boston, Massachusetts where one member was eating a bloody heart, symbolic of President Trump's heart! Many young people have turned against God, love, and compassion to hate, violence, and satanism. Violence has erupted with BLM (Black Lives Matter) groups and they are now talking about anarchy and killing whites. On Instagram, someone posted art depicting two overweight black women, naked, and holding two white severed heads.

How can people be this hateful and lacking spirituality? It's called programming. The planners of this evil coup know how impressionable young minds are, and most of humanity.

Such horrible images are a frightening reminder of Hitler's Nazi Germany and the unimaginable horror perpetrated on the Jewish people during World War II. Some Americans are mentally deranged humans. And we wonder why aliens won't contact us. We are too violent.

Time traveler John Titor's warned us from his future that a horrible civil war took place in the United States beginning in 2011 but he also said that a timeline can be altered and what happened to his world might not happen in ours. But here we are, and it appears that the same events that happened in his parallel world will take place in our time—2021.

For those who don't know the story, John Titor claimed to be from the year 2036, sixteen years in our future time while he answered questions on an internet blog in the year 2000. John spent four months answering every kind of question put to him and included photographs of his time machine and an operation manual. People began asking about the physics of time travel, why he was here, and what he thought of our society. Many dismissed the condescending and sometimes peevish answers by John, while others were angered or frightened by his tantalizing answers to many subjects and his predictions.

If John was a hoaxer, he certainly was a great actor and well-versed on a large number of subjects. I, for one, believe the story might have validity, especially in light of American physicist Hugh Everett's (November 11, 1930-July 19, 1982) many-world interpretation of quantum physics and the experiments that prove there might be many unseen levels to our existence even a parallel universe.

Titor was asked if some sort of new world government was in place by 2011. And John's response was, "On my worldline, in 2011, the United States is in the middle of a civil war that has dramatic effects on most of the Western governments."

Does that mean a N.W.O. (New World Order) government is coming? God help us if it does become our reality.

Titor claimed that whenever he jumped into a new timeline events changed. At our present time of 2020, a revolution began the day George Floyd, a black man, was killed by police on May 25,

2020. A group known as BLM (Black Lives Matters) sprang into existence. Although Black Lives Matter claim they are a social movement advocating for non-violent civil disobedience in protest against incidents of police brutality and all racially motivated violence against black people, that isn't what happened. Instead, night after night riots rages in large cities across America. Businesses both owned by both white and black owners were looted and burned. I have seen a YouTube video of a black woman claiming to be a Marxist and how "her people" plan to bring down America any way necessary.

John said this about his youth. "In the year 2012, I was 14 years old spending most of my time living, running, and hiding in the woods and rivers of central Florida. The civil war was in its 7th year and the world war was three years away. The next time John was asked what started the civil war he answered the civil war will be started between the Democrats and Republicans.

Could a civil war in American in 2020 continue into the year 2027? I can't imagine that with the military getting involved to stop the rioting and violence.

Since Obama was elected the Democrats and Republications in Congress have shown little or no bipartisanship. Many issues and bills remain in limbo even for Trump's administration. Perhaps events will unfold that will prevent a civil war at the last minute, but I don't see it that way. I see bloodshed and burning in the cities after November 3, 2020.

John referred to our current society and seemed to see our world as beyond help when he stated, "Have you considered that your society might be better off if half of you were dead? While you sit by and watch your Constitution being torn away from you, you willfully eat poisoned food, buy manufactured products no one needs, and turn an uncaring eye away from millions of people suffering and dying all around you. Is this the 'Universal Law' you subscribe to?"

John showed more disdain for our society when he said, "Perhaps I should let you all in on a little secret. No one likes you in the future. This time is looked at as being full of lazy, self-centered, civically ignorant sheep. Perhaps you should be less concerned about me and more concerned about that!"

Ouch! Titor was right about the majority of humans on planet Earth. After watching the debates between Trump and Biden and Kamala Harris and VP Mike Pence, I am astonished by man's inhumanity to each other with the evil rhetoric, the hate, the vindictiveness, and lack of compassion shown on social media. After Trump went into the hospital for COVID, people were on Twitter and other social media wishing he were dead. Who raised these horrible humans, and do they have a soul? Were they ever taught to "Judge not lest ye be judged," or "Do unto others as you would like them to do to you?" What these people don't realize that there is a universal Karma, and what you put out into the Universe, will come back to you, whether positive or negative.

Here's another possibility and I realize it's far out, but two Native American men interviewed with author Dr. Ardy Clarke in her book, *Encounters With Star People.*, They had witnessed large craft hovering over their Southwestern reservations unloading clones humans. In one instant, the Native American, Willie Joe, watched these oddly dressed human-looking beings in older clothing. He described one woman seemed to have trouble walking in high heels. They got into an older car and started leaving the reservation but didn't get far with a flat tire. Willie Joe went to help, and they seemed perplexed about changing a tire as if they had never seen one changed. He told them he needed to jack up the car to change the tire, and they need to get out of the car. He said it was if they didn't understand the instructions. As soon as the spare tire was on the car, the driver handed Willie Joe, ten silver dollars, a rare find.

Both Native American men said that they have seen their doubles, but they are not them, and they thought that the clone beings don't have souls like humans. Are there millions of these cloned beings in our cities now and are they here to create the riots and other events that are unfolding.

I must add this—please do not harm anyone because of this story. It may be fiction. We don't need more excuses for violence in our world.

The future and past may be far more fluid and malleable than we think. In John's parallel universe, another Civil War occurred in the United States and World War III was a part of history, but in our current reality, it has not happened, and hopefully, it will never happen. But he did say that the civil war sometime in our time that was instigated by the Democrats and the Republicans. And look at all the verbal abuse they are slinging at each other over the impeachment of Donald Trump. Could this be the beginning of the Civil War that John had read about in his history books?

Already violent protests are taking place in U.S. cities where burning, looting, and often deaths have occurred. Will this get worse? I foresee two huge explosions taking place in a large city near a bridge sometime before the end of 2020 or early 2021. It seems terrorist related. Many cities have bridges, but I sense it might involve either—London or San Francisco.

John may have given us a glimmer of hope by stating that timelines can be changed, and nothing is set in stone. *En masse* human consciousness can alter events and timelines, but are there enough human beings to create the *Butterfly in the Hurricane?* This is the idea that small causes may have large effects.

2021 Looking into The Future

CHAPTER TWENTY-ONE

SPACE ANGELS

For most humans on this planet, they have a narrow view of other intelligent species that live outside our planet or even it our planet. In the coming years, our eyes will be opened to be intelligence throughout the solar system and the universe. Consider this story that was included in my book, *Extraterrestrial Encounters of the Extraordinary Kind* © 2020.

Not only have American astronauts seen anomalous things in space, but Russian cosmonauts have reported sightings they can't rationally explain. It was July 1984, and the Soviet space program was at its peak when an unexpected event occurred at the Salyut-7 space station that Russian authorities decided not to mention.

On July 12, 1984, three veteran cosmonauts, Leonid Kizim, Oleg Atkov, and Vladimir Solovyov, were part of a 155-day mission and engaged in unknown programmed experiments. This was the day the group reported strange orange lights and beings. According to the three cosmonauts, the space station was completely bathed in a mesmerizing orange light. It appeared to enter from outside the space station and bled through an opaque wall.

For a short time, the orange light was so bright that it blinded the crew. When their vision returned, they all looked out the portholes for the source of the light, looking for a possible explosion on their space station. The Salyut 7 had already suffered previous fires, but what the crew saw was more unfathomable than the orange light.

All of the cosmonauts reported seeing seven huge angel-like beings who hovered outside the space station. They were seven of them, at least 80 feet tall, with a humanoid appearance—face and bodies that appeared human, but they also had wings and halos. These beings kept pace with the space station for at least 10-minutes before vanishing from sight.

On day 167, the crew was then joined by another team of three cosmonauts from the Soyuz T-12 spacecraft—Svetlana Savitskaya, Igor Volk, and Vladimir Dzhanibekov. Shortly after joining the original cosmonauts, the Salyut 7 was once again bathed in a warm orange light. Then, like clockwork, they immediately looked out the portholes, and again, they were joined by angelic beings.

All of the cosmonauts agreed the beings were the size of an "airliner." The incident was deemed top secret by the old Soviet Union and the crew was cautioned not to speak of the event publicly.

How could six cosmonauts witness the same extraordinary event in space? The events were dismissed as fatigue due to the cosmonauts extended stay in space or due to oxygen deprivation. After this strange incident, the crew went on to stay in the vessel for a record-breaking 237 days before abandoning it.

These beings appeared different from normal human beings, not only because of their enormous wings or the dazzling halo around their heads, but the main difference was the expression on their faces. "They smiled at us," the cosmonauts later declared. And they added, "It was not a smile of greeting, but a smile of joy!"

Thoughts on the Event

Isn't it interesting that the space station was numbered 7 and there were 7 angelic beings seen by the crew? The number seven is an angelic number, and it is used 635 times in the Bible. When the flight directors read the report of what the cosmonauts had seen, they immediately recorded it as *"top secret,"* ordering the cosmonauts themselves and the medical staff who followed them not to mention the incident. At the time, the existence of angels was not permitted by Soviet communist ideology. Later, after the fall of the Berlin Wall and the end of the Cold War, it was discovered that even some American astronauts repeatedly encountered angels in space.

Angels in Space by U.S. Astronauts

The cosmonauts were not the only ones to encounter angels in space. Not long ago, the Western media published sensational photographs made by the Hubble telescope showing strange images included what looked like human-like winged silhouettes. Researchers were especially interested in the series of photos made on Earth's orbit. One could make out seven luminous objects on them. John Pratchett, an engineer for the Hubble project, said that he had seen those creatures himself.

It was also said that U.S. astronauts onboard NASA's space shuttles also encountered angel-like creatures. On December 26, 1994, the Hubble telescope transmitted hundreds of photos depicting a large white city floating in space. U.S authorities did not expose the photos to the general public, of course, although it was rumored that U.S. officials treated NASA's report very seriously.

Also, a Russian cosmonaut who spent six months living and working onboard the Mir Space Station said that he and his partner had experienced fantastic visions from time to time. It seemed to the men that they were turning into other creatures—other people or animals, and even humanoids of extraterrestrial origin.

Similar stories are often told by aircraft pilots. It is known as the phenomenon of a giant hand. As a rule, the phenomenon occurs during long-lasting flights. When it happens, a pilot feels that the control wheel is being grasped by someone's invisible hand. Researchers from the U.S. Air Force concluded that nearly 15 percent of pilots have experienced the effect during their work. It has not been ruled out that the giant hand phenomenon is behind many air crashes.

NASA psychologists speculate that such factors as pressure and temperature fluctuations and shortage of oxygen might explain hallucinations of the giant hand phenomenon. Or could it involve an unknown psychic force?

CHAPTER TWENTY-TWO

GOVERNMENT EXPERIMENTS

The most frightening part of this story, if true, is that our own scientists and military allow such horrific experiments on unsuspecting citizens. Many of these people might be some of the millions of missing people reported worldwide. The stories are reminiscent of the evil experiments Nazis performed on the Jewish people—women, children, and men, during World War II.

If you think our government or military is incapable of such brutality, think again. History is full of their experiments on unwilling victims—such as:

- Tuskegee Syphilis Study on African American males from 1932 to 1972 by the U.S. Public Health Service.
- Project MK Ultra Mind Control and Project Monarch experiments involving children and adults using the covert administration of high doses of psychoactive

drugs (LSD) and other chemicals, electroshock, hypnosis, sensory deprivation, isolation, verbal and sexual abuse, as well as other forms of torture. Refer to *Trace Formation of America* book by Cathy O'Brien and her handler Mark Phillips.

- In 1966, the U.S. Army released Bacillus globigii into the tunnels of the New York City Subway system, as part of a field experiment called A Study of the Vulnerability of Subway Passengers in New York City to Covert Attack with Biological Agents.

- Atom and nuclear testing on hundreds of military men who were not warned of the danger of radiation.

- Threats of chemical and biological warfare led the U.S. Department of Defense to start "Project 112" from 1963 to the early 1970s. Part of the effort involved spraying different ships and hundreds of Navy sailors with nerve agents such as sarin and VX, in order to test the effectiveness of decontamination procedures and safety measures at the time. The Pentagon revealed the details of the Project Shipboard Hazard and Defense (SHAD) project in 2002, and the Veterans Administration began studying possible health effects among sailors who participated in SHAD. This was just one of many chemical warfare experiments conducted by the U.S. military, starting with volunteer tests involving mustard gas in World War II.

I could continue with the list of atrocities, but I think you get the picture that our government doesn't really care about us and what experiments they conduct on its citizens. We are guinea pigs for military and certain aliens.

CHAPTER TWENTY-THREE

MYSTERY DRONES

December of 2019 and January of 2020, the plains of rural northeastern Colorado and southwestern Nebraska were the epicenter of sightings of what appeared to be unidentified drones. Despite the media attention and the speculation that they were related to the security forces responsible for protecting intercontinental ballistic missile silos scattered throughout the region, military bases in the area denied that the drones were theirs.

While the mystery of the drones' operator or operators still remains unsolved, a series of internal emails obtained through the Freedom of Information Act reveal just how serious the drone reports were taken by the 90th Security Forces Group and the public affairs office at F.E. Warren Air Force Base. The emails are heavily redacted, but they at least shed some light on the confusion even the base experienced at the hands of this bizarre mystery.

In late December 2019, *The War Zone* was among the first outlets to report on the somewhat bizarre story of fleets of unidentified drones operating in the airspace above northeastern Colorado and western Nebraska. There was a sense of near-panic as law enforcement agencies were inundated with scores of reports of these drones, prompting the creation of a task force that included the FAA, federal law enforcement agencies like the FBI, and sheriffs from multiple Colorado counties. Eventually, the State of Colorado sent one of its well-equipped surveillance planes to hunt for the drones. Since then, however, reports of suspicious drone activity have dropped significantly, according to the Colorado Department of Public Safety and Nebraska State Patrol.

Despite the large effort and the mobilization of Colorado's infrared camera-equipped aircraft, nothing conclusive was identified and, to date, no one has come forward to claim responsibility for the drone activities. That doesn't mean that the case was closed, however.

Not only was there confusion within the agency, but multiple highly credible official reports from trained observers from the timeframe when the objects were present in the region. Many of them match to a remarkable degree and they allude to a unique arrangement in which a large drone seems to have been accompanied by a fleet of smaller ones.

Douglas D. Johnson, a volunteer researcher operating in affiliation with the Scientific Coalition for UAP Studies (SCU), recently obtained emails through the Freedom of Information Act (FOIA) which catalog the internal communications of the public affairs office at F.E. Warren and the 90th Security Forces Group regarding the spate of drone sightings. The 90th Security Forces Group provides security both for F.E. Warren and the 150 Minuteman III Intercontinental ballistic missiles (ICBMs) operated by the 90th Missile Wing.

Johnson filed two separate FOIA requests for all official correspondence to and from Jon Carkhuff, a public affairs officer and spokesman associated with F.E. Warren Air Force Base, and all official correspondence to and from the headquarters staff of the 90th Security Forces Group that contain any of the following terms: drone, drones, counter-drone, counter-drones, unmanned aerial system, unmanned aerial systems, UAS, counter-UAS, unidentified aircraft, unidentified aerial, unidentified flying, unknown aircraft, UFO, and anomalous. The FOIA requests were for communications ranging from December 15, 2019, through January 18, 2020. The requests were filed on January 18, 2020 and were fulfilled on February 14.

Many parts of the communications Johnson received are redacted, including the names of the participants in the email chains in which the mystery drones and the base's response to media inquiries about them are discussed. In an exchange about how to respond to an early media inquiry, an unknown sender writes, "We need to ensure he doesn't feel like we are hiding anything." On the next page in the same release, after a statement "we do not know the origin of the drones," one writer inserted the hashtag "aliens."

As the FOIA documents show, public affairs staff at F.E. Warren would eventually release an official press statement on January 17 after receiving input from Major General Ferdinand 'Fred' B. Stoss III, commander of 20th Air Force, the part of Air Force Global Strike Command responsible for overseeing the entire ICBM force. The final version of the statement that was released states definitively that F.E. Warren was not responsible for the drones:

We can confirm that the drones spotted in Colorado and Nebraska are not from F.E. Warren Air Force Base and are not affiliated in any way with the United States Air Force. We have provided this information to the FAA, FBI, and state and local authorities, as they investigate this matter.

The drones have not posed a threat to any of our sites, facilities, or operations. F.E. Warren AFB does conduct counter-UAS training within the confines of the installation, however, any drones spotted outside of the installation are not part of our fleet.

Aside from discussions and drafts pertaining to the production of that official statement, the FOIA releases contain entire emails that are redacted and seem to have once contained nothing, but images of drones taken by eyewitnesses. The only images not redacted are a series taken by a Nebraska State Trooper.

Despite being heavily censored, the emails reveal that many at F.E. Warren were just as confused by the mystery drones as the public was.

In one email contained in the F.E. Warren public affairs office FOIA release, the palpable confusion of staff can be detected in the fact that there seems to be no agreement on who might be responsible for the drone sightings. "[Redacted] — understand you're part of the FBI TF [task force] looking at this? Pls send me an update," the email reads. "This is becoming a bigger deal. What's our PA [public affairs] play here right now WRT [with regards to] this (ongoing drone) effort?"

In another email sent on January 2, 2020, an unknown sender notes the bewilderment the region experienced at the height of the drone panic:

Hey colonel:

Northeastern Colorado is in a tizzy about drone sightings. They all seem clustered in an area that has quite a few Minuteman sites. Do you know if security forces are playing with UASs [unmanned aircraft systems] up there?

An email within the 90th Security Forces Group FOIA release dated January 8, 2020 states that the drones are "100000000000% not us." I've seen some articles pointing the finger as us [sic]," the sender writes, "but I can definitely say this is not our team."

Even the Air Force Office of Special Investigations (AFOSI) got involved with the drone mystery. AFOSI is military law enforcement and investigative agency that reports directly to the Secretary of the Air Force whose stated mission is to "identify, exploit and neutralize criminal, terrorist, and intelligence threats in multiple domains to the Air Force, Department of Defense and U.S. Government." Its stated capabilities are to detect threats, conduct investigations, and "protect secrets."

A 90th Security Forces Group email dated January 6, 2020, adds that the sender will "defer to [Redacted] on this one since AFOSI is the lead agency on the FEW [F.E. Warren AFB] side for this issue." In a separate email within the FOIA release from the public affairs office at F.E. Warren, it is written that the AFOSI would send a representative to the closed-door task force meeting held on Jan. 6 in Brush, Colorado.

Several of the emails in the 90th Security Forces Group FOIA release mention AF/A10, the office of the U.S. Air Force Air Staff that oversees Strategic Deterrence and Nuclear Integration.

"AF/A10 reached down asked for confirmation that we (AFSGC) [Air Force Global Strike Command] are not flying the drones in question," one email reads.

In one of the stranger exchanges found in the 90th Security Forces Group release, a participant in the email chain writes that some eyewitness reports state that the drones were dropping what appeared to be "potatoes" and that the Perkins County Sheriff's Office collected some of them for analysis:

Sheriff's deputies are responding and seeing the drones as well. They reported seeing a "mothership" 6' in diameter flanked by 10 smaller drones (some fixed-wing, some not). When deputies follow the drones, they clock them at speeds of 60-70 mph. The drones also appear to be dropping or picking up things that look like "potatoes" [Redacted]

The FBI in Colorado and the Joint Terrorism Task Force (JTTF) in Omaha are currently looking into the sightings. Perkins County Sherriff's [sic] Office has three of the potatoes frozen in storage and will likely transfer them to the FBI for analysis. The FAA is sending an agent to Colorado this upcoming weekend to help investigate and handle the news coverage.

In an email dated January 2, someone else in the email chain added that "The "potatoes" have an agricultural purpose and are used by farmers with their large center-pivot irrigation systems." *The Denver Post* identified the "potatoes" as SOILPAM Tracklogs, a tool used to help fill the ruts left by wheels on large irrigation systems.

The FAA concluded that mysterious drone reports in northeast Colorado and parts of Nebraska posed no threat to military operations and at no time intruded on restricted airspace. But they have no idea where they came from or why they were there.

Sixteen counties had at least one sighting by a law enforcement official, according to the documents. The sightings reports were consistent, describing a large drone, approximately 6 feet in length. Some reports indicated the large drone was accompanied by a fleet of as many as a dozen small drones. Who has access to six-foot drones—certainly not potato farmers! It's highly unlikely that potato farmers were involved with a fleet of highly sophisticated drones for their Tracklogs.

Early reports described the drones flying in a "grid pattern," as if they were mapping the area. Concern grew over the drones' proximity to ICBM silos in the region, and an Air Force base in Wyoming.

Surely, the FBI and those involved in the investigation would have uncovered the source of the drones by now. For some time around Christmas 2019 and New Year's 2020, something unexplained was happening over the Colorado Plains. So mysterious that the federal government's own agency tasked with regulating the skies over the United States still has no clue what exactly took place or who was behind it.

Palo Verde Drones over Nuclear Power Plants

In the past year, strange unidentified craft with unexplainable capabilities began appearing over extremely sensitive United States installations. On the evening of September in 2019 America's most powerful nuclear plant at Palo Verde situated approximately 56 miles west of Phoenix, near Tonopah, Arizona experienced a swarm of drones over this area.

In a volume of documents and internal correspondences related to the event, officials from the Nuclear Regulatory Commission (NRC) described the incident as a "drone-a-palooza" and said that it highlighted concerns about the potential for a future "adversarial attack" involving small unmanned aircraft and the need for defenses against them. Even so, the helplessness and even cavalier attitude toward the drone incident as it was unfolding by those that are tasked with securing one of America's largest and most sensitive nuclear facilities serves as an alarming and glaring example of how neglected and misunderstood this issue is.

This is what a security officer reported:

"On 9/30/19 at approximately 2051 hours, it was reported by a Security Team Leader that Unmanned Aerial Vehicles (UAVs) were approaching the plant from the east (true east). The hours of darkness made it difficult to estimate the altitude at which the UAVs were flying. Two Security Team Leaders [redacted]. The UAVs appeared to have been launching from behind the mountain range at the intersection of Southern Ave and 361 Ave just east of the plant. Four UAVs were confirmed to have been spotted at one time flying northwest over Unit 1 and returning northeast over Unit 3. LLEA (MCSO) [Maricopa County Sheriff's Office] deputies were dispatched to the area of the mountain range with a Security Unit Team Leader in an attempt to determine the location of the UAV operators but were unsuccessful. No other UAVs were observed after approximately 2300 hours."

"These UAVs are believed to have been the same UAVs that flew over the plant the night before on 9/29/19 at approximately 2020 hours."

"All required notifications were made IAW [in accordance with] 20DP-0SK49 Security Integrated Response Plan and additional Security contingency measure [sic] were implemented IAW 21SP-0SK11 Security Contingencies."

Were terrorists collecting information for an attack on our nuclear plants or alien drones scouting our nuclear facilities? The reason I included this information is that there are a great many reports of UFO sightings and their ability to shape-shift from airplanes to helicopters. The U.S. Army's Dugway Proving Ground in Northern Utah, also known as the New Area 51, continues to be a hot spot of unidentified flying objects. Robert Saxon, Dugway's chief of public relations, discounts the UFO reports as testing at Dugway that goes on 24-hours each day and how car lights from a distance can appear ufo-ish.

2021 Looking into The Future

CHAPTER TWENTY-FOUR

UFOs, PRESIDENTS, AND POLITICIANS

July 2020, United States Senator Marco Rubio (R-FL) was interviewed by an investigative reporter who works for the CBS television station in Miami this week. In this interview, the reporter, Jim DeFede, asked Senator Rubio, "Are we alone?"

To which, Senator Rubio gives a lengthy answer. "Here's the interesting thing for me about all this. And the reason why I think it's an important topic, okay. And that is we have things flying over our military bases and places where we're conducting military exercises, and we don't know what it is, and it isn't ours. So that's the legitimate question to ask. I would say that, frankly, that if it's something outside from outside this planet, that might be better than the fact that we've seen some technological leap on behalf of the Chinese or the Russians or some other adversary that allows them to conduct this sort of activity. But the bottom line is, there are things flying over your military bases, and you don't know what they are, because they're not yours. And they exhibit technologies that you don't have at your own disposal. That to me is a national security risk and one that we should be looking into. And so that's the premise I begin with."

Jim DeFede: "Let's clear this up, who would be looking into this and they would be generating some sort of a publicly available report. And you're not using the phrase unidentified flying objects, you have another euphemism for it, unidentified aerial phenomenon."

Sen. Marco Rubio: "I didn't, I didn't come up with. That's the one that the military uses internally. And ultimately, you know that that's the one we use, then what we're saying, Yeah, so the Office of Naval Intelligence, this is over, has impacted the Navy for the most part. I've seen reports on this now for the better part of a decade. Other countries have had similar reports. Our perspective, is, there's someone flying in the airspace that no one else is allowed to fly in, and we don't know who it is, and it isn't something we have. We need to know what that is. I mean, that's in my mind. I mean, that's I don't understand why we wouldn't want to know what it is. Maybe there's a completely sort of boring explanation for it. But we need to find out. And so that's really what we're asking about, and we're asking him to make public as much as possible that information, none of that really fits into the mold of classified per se."

Jim DeFede: "All right, but so what's your gut? Are we alone in the universe or is there something else out there?"

Sen. Marco Rubio: "I don't have a gut feeling about it because it's a phenomenon. It's unexplained. I go, I just want to know what it is and if we can't determine what it is, and that's a fact what we need to take into account. I wouldn't venture to speculate beyond that."

On November 26, 2019, what was described as a "slow-moving blob" on radar triggered a lockdown of the White House and caused the US Capitol to be placed on "restrictive access." Senior national security officials across the agencies convened to coordinate and monitor the situation after the mysterious "blob" was seen on radar at the Capitol Police command center flying just south of the National Mall, according to a law enforcement source. Military aircraft were scrambled in response.

The initial assessments indicated that the "blob" was an unauthorized aircraft entering restrictive airspace, leading to the brief lockdown. The airspace around Washington is more restricted than anywhere else in the country, according to the FAA, as "rules put in place after the 9/11 attacks establish 'national defense airspace' over the area and limit aircraft operations to those with an FAA and Transportation Security Administration authorization."

"Senior officials across the interagency are monitoring the situation on a national event conference call. NORAD aircraft was on site. "A plane is not considered hostile at this time," Pentagon spokesman Lt. Col. Chris Mitchell said during the early stages of the event. But hours after "the all-clear" was given, a defense official told CNN that a final determination had not yet been made as to what exactly caused the event.

Did a UFO buzz the White House on November 26, 2019, like the headline reports of "flying saucers" buzzing the White House in 1952 on several occasions?

President Trump seems to be giving us lots of hints about the future. December of 2019 President Trump signed a $738 billion defense spending bill to creating the official Space Force. It's the sixth branch of the U.S. Armed Services, and the first new military service since the Air Force was created in 1947.

"Space is the world's newest war-fighting domain," President Trump said during the signing ceremony." Amid grave threats to our national security, American superiority in space is absolutely vital. And we're leading, but we're not leading by enough. But very shortly we'll be leading by a lot."

Does Trump feel a War in space is coming? Will the Space Force fight humans or aliens in the future?

Also, President Trump made this statement during his speech at the World Economic Forum in Davos, Switzerland on January 20, 2020. *The great scientific breakthroughs of the 20th century —from penicillin to high-yield wheat, to modern transportation, and breakthrough vaccines — have lifted living standards and saved billions of lives around the world. And we're continuing to work on things that you'll be hearing about in the near future that, even today, sitting here right now, you wouldn't believe it's possible that we have found the answers. You'll be hearing about it. But we have found answers to things that people said would not be possible — certainly not in a very short period of time.*

But the wonders of the last century will pale in comparison to what today's young innovators will achieve because they are doing things that nobody thought even feasible to begin. We continue to embrace technology, not to shun it. When people are free to innovate, millions will live longer, happier, healthier lives.

Trump's speech almost sounds like a hint that our technology is far more advanced than we can imagine—could it be advanced weapons, unimaginable spacecraft, or even time travel?

With the top-secret UFO information recently released in 2020 by the Pentagon, President Donald Trump said that he had watched the footage from the Pentagon showing "unidentified aerial phenomena" and called it a "hell of a video" but he wonders "if it's real."

Then on June 9, 2020, President Donald Trump told his son Donald Trump Jr. in a televised interview hosted by the President's reelection campaign, that he heard some interesting things about Roswell. In the interview on Father's Day. Don Jr. asked his father if he would work to gather more information on the event [Roswell] "and let us know what's really going on."

"I won't talk to you about what I know about it, but it's very interesting," President Trump replied.

Donald Trump Jr. then asked, "Will you let us know if there's aliens?

President Trump's response was, "So many people ask me that question."

When asked if he would declassify the information he's referring to, Trump said, "Well, I'll have to think about that one."

The President in the past has spoken skeptically about the possibility that there is something (aliens) out there. Last year, Trump said he received a short briefing on UFO sightings, but also offered, "People are saying they're seeing UFOs. Do I believe it? Not particularly."

President Ronald Reagan on an outside threat

During the 1985 Geneva Summit high-level diplomatic talks, United States President Ronald Reagan and the leader of the Soviet Union Mikhail Gorbachev took a short break from the ongoing negotiations to go for a walk, accompanied only by their private interpreters. The two leaders, each in control of the most powerful militaries on the globe at the time and actively working to prevent a nuclear war that could mean the end of all humanity, walked and talked in secrecy, and not sharing details of their conversation until decades later. In 2009, the subject of their short conversation finally came to light.

Reagan seemed to have more than a nuclear threat on his mind—it was something out of this world. During a 2009 interview with news reporter Charlie Rose and Reagan's Secretary of State, George Shultz, Rose asked what the two leaders discussed as they walked and talked in private. Shultz said, "From the fireside house, President Reagan suddenly said this about his conversation with Gorbachev. "What would you do if the United States were suddenly attacked by someone from outer space? Would you help us?"

Gorbachev said, "No doubt about it."

Reagan replied, "We too. So that's interesting."

Reagan also gave a very odd speech at the United Nations on September 21, 1987, and said, "Perhaps we need some outside universal threat to make us recognize this common bond. I occasionally think how quickly our differences worldwide would vanish if we were facing an alien threat from outside this world."

President Truman on Aliens

Thirty-third United States President Harry Truman purportedly authorized "Operation Majestic Twelve" in 1947. If the secret committee is known as the Majestic 12 ever really existed, this is the day that the group was allegedly created by a memorandum from President Harry Truman.

If real, this clandestine bunch of scientists, military brass, and government officials came together in response to the Army's recovery of an alien spacecraft that crashed on a ranch near Roswell, New Mexico, in July 1947, then what was their purpose? It seems it was to investigate the circumstances surrounding the Roswell incident and to maintain vigilance against further alien incursions. If the secret committee is known as the Majestic 12 ever existed, this is the day, September 24, 1947, that the group was allegedly created by a memorandum from President Harry Truman.

Confirming the existence of MJ-12 is central to the argument by UFO conspiracy theorists that the U.S. government has deliberately hidden UFO information from the public ever since Roswell. The government appears committed to keeping the public in the dark about aliens. Presidents tease about them, but no one will come forward with the truth, and I am sure they known.

But one of these days a fleet of UFOs will land in Washington, D.C., and then how will they explain them away—mass hallucination?

CHAPTER TWENTY-FIVE

REFLECTIONS

My dear mentor and long-time friend, a registered Oglala Sioux Ceremonial Leader and author, Ed McGaa aka "Eagle Man" (1936-2017) said, "We have strayed from our Natural Path. Our rich ancestral wisdoms from the tribal peoples of Europe, centuries past, and those of us who are Indigenous, more recently, are in danger of being lost, plunging us into chaos and despair as we tear ourselves from the energy that created and sustains us."

Ed often talked to me about overpopulation and his dire vision of what was to come. He said, "The number One forthcoming disaster is overpopulation—and anyone who disputes this man-created happening is a sheer idiot."

Ed never minced his words and I respected him that.

Over seven billion currently inhabit the Earth, and soon there will be eight billion. He worried about food and the destruction of our environment. He worried, as I do, about how our planet is in serious danger. Ed said, "Without a livable environment, Spirituality and Organized Religion will be short-lived. Man is foolish, actually, totally disloyal to the human race and the animal brethren, to disregard the warnings of science.".

Ed wrote about the pine beetle's destruction of ancient pine trees, the unpredictable weather and extreme temperatures, the pollution of our precious waters, and the coming droughts. Glaciers are melting worldwide, icebergs are melting, the permafrost is melting and causing increased methane in the air. In Russia, methane has exploded underground and caused huge holes in the ground. On June 20, 2020, Siberia hit a record-breaking temperature of 100 degrees Fahrenheit, the hottest temperature ever recorded in the Arctic region.

I attended several of Ed's ceremonies and a sweat lodge ceremony in Ketchum, Idaho in 1992. Ed didn't think much of organized religion because it didn't really honor the Creator and all the Creator's work. Indigenous people are taught to honor the four directions and elements, the trees, the birds, the four-leggeds, the finned ones, the insects, and the rocks.

If you watched James Cameron's beautiful 2009 movie, *Avatar*, you can see the similarity between the *Na'vi* of Pandora and the Indigenous people on Earth. There was a biological network on Pandora where everything is connected. Writer/Director James Cameron understands this connection and this movie was a powerful lesson about our connection to all life on Earth.

Sadly, we have separated ourselves from our planet. In the movie there a quote by the hero Jake Sully who recounts what Neytiri has told him about the *Na'vi* way of life. "She said all energy is only borrowed, and one day you have to give it back."

Some claimed the movie promoted the worship of nature, which they say is a false God. That's is ludicrous! Cameron's religious critics suggest the Bible offers a much deeper portrayal of the true monotheistic God. I had this discussion with a cousin in Houston, Texas, a Baptist. She felt that my book, *Earth Energy*, was promoting a false god because I said that the Creator is in everything. How utterly ridiculous and narrow-minded! In Genesis, it described how God created the Universe and Earth—right? That means that God's energy moves through all life and even inanimate objects in our world. How can we separate ourselves from this energy which is pervasive in our world and throughout the Universe?

That's the problem with our world—we don't see the connection we have with our living, breathing planet, and until we awaken to this connection, we will feel lost.

We forget how special our planet is in the solar system. So far NASA has not found a planet that contains water like Earth or life. Gaia or Earth is unique and fragile. People who have remote viewed other planets have seen entire civilizations that were destroyed— either by their own technology or a natural event. Science tells us that the dinosaurs were wiped out 65 million years ago by an asteroid. It could happen to us and this time it might be by extraterrestrials who think that we are beyond redemption. Each day should be counted as a blessing even during the time of COVID-19. Humans take everything for granted and mistakenly believe that our way of life will last forever. Don't count on it!

The Crop Circle Message to Humanity

Question: Are the crop circles worldwide created by humans or otherworldly beings?

Answer: Actually, both. Skeptics often point to two older men, Doug Bower and Dave Choley, who started making crop circles in England during the 1970s, but the joke was on them. Many of the circles would have been impossible to create by two men or other people using just a board pushing down the crops. Some formations are intricate. The one thing that always differentiated the hoaxer circles from the unknown creators was the hoaxers always damage the crops while the unknown crop circles creators are never damaged. There is a disagreement on how far the crop circles go back in time. Some stories go back as 1678, and I don't think Doug and Dave were alive back then.

Another interesting aspect of the crop circles has been the orbs and UFOs witnessed and filmed over the farmer's field where a crop circle was being created.

The crop circles have bewildered the British since the 1600s, which have since spread to Europe, Russia, North America, Japan, and India. The complexity of the designs—many of which have a mathematical basis. Crop circles have escalated in the past two decades, reflecting a serious and science-literate artistic movement. Mathematics is central to the modern designs, which incorporate symbols and fundamental constants such as ϕ — the 'golden ratio' and π, sometimes to an accuracy of ten digits. Thanks to increased computing power, iterative equations are used to generate shapes that repeat across many scales. Pictographs today can measure 300 meters across and can comprise up to 2,000 elements.

In 2020, several crop circles appeared with amazing complexity. The crop circle below was discovered in Ammersee (South End, West of Munich, Bavaria, Germany on July 26, 2020. The crop circle appears to be woven to create a three-dimensional appearance.

Crop Circle discovered July 26, 2020, near Munich, Germany

On May 28, 2020, the crop circle below appeared near Potterne Field, near Devizes, Wiltshire, United Kingdom, resembling the Coronavirus with an extension.

Crop circle discovered on May 28, 2020, in the UK

Then August 8, 2020 (8-8-2020), one of the last crop circles to appear in the UK for the year appeared to be connected to the May 28, 2020 crop circle that looked like the Coronavirus.

Several people hypothesized that a far more important message was being conveyed by benevolent aliens. They believed the first crop circle on May 28, 2020, represented the Coronavirus but wondered if the strange protrusion was depicting a "spike 8 protein." The one created on August 8, 2020, they believed felt represented a molecule or a hydrocarbon, which is a naturally occurring compound consisting only of hydrogen and carbon. It exists everywhere in the Universe.

An unnamed professor of chemistry at an undisclosed university was contacted and said the formation was a "unique" hydrocarbon. Some ufologists felt the crop circle formation represented the drug II-IV (2-4) Dimethyl-III-Isopropyl-pentane, known to fight viruses, which is also used to treat epilepsy cases.

Did advanced spiritual aliens create both crop circles to assist us from the deadly virus that has spread worldwide? What crop circle maker (human) would know about the hydrocarbon that the professor referred to as "unique?" What if the spike protein was added to the (2-4) Dimethyl-III-Isopropyl-pentane, could it be the answer to the world's horrible pandemic?

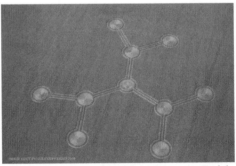

August 8, 2020 Crop Circle at Patney Bridge, UK

Already scientists are looking into viral spike protein antigens that are possible candidates for a vaccine. Could a simple pill be the answer to the virus instead of millions or billions of vaccines?

Without a doubt, there are incredible beings out there who want to help us, if we listen. Unfortunately, greed always wins out and those who run the world won't allow it. That's the way it has always been with inventions that could change our world and clean up our oceans, skies, and land with free energy that exists everywhere.

Nikola Tesla knew about free energy that is found throughout our universe, but his papers and writings were seized after his death on January 7, 1943. Nikola Tesla's attempt to provide everyone in the world with free energy with his World Power System, a method of broadcasting electrical energy without wires, through the ground that was never finished.

Our world would be a far better place with free energy.

Time Travelers

Question: You have written about time travel, but do you believe it exists now?

Answer: There seems to be an abundance of extraterrestrials visiting Earth, and some ufologists have speculated they are time travelers from Earth's future. Time travelers are certainly a possibility, and there have been rumors the CERN and the United States military have used time travel for the past 50 years.

Compared to the ET and ancient alien books, very little has been written on the possibility of Earth-born human beings traveling from the far or near future to their past (our timeline) or visiting in the distant past to alter the future. And if time travel is possible, does a timeline change each time someone leaps into another timeline?

In Einstein's theory of gravity and general relativity—space and time are merged as spacetime, which allows for the possibility of pathways that could bend back to the past and loop back to the future. Several candidate theories have been developed for merging general relativity and quantum mechanics into a unified theory. It's an open question whether these candidates would allow time travel like the way general relativity does.

The mechanism for traveling into the distant future is to use the time-dilation effect of Special Relativity, which states that a moving clock appears to tick more slowly the closer it approaches the speed of light. This effect, which has been overwhelmingly supported by experimental tests, applies to all types of clocks, including biological aging.

If the story of the Philadelphia Experiment was true back in 1943, then our military has probably advanced in the technology of time travel. Allegedly, in the fall of 1943, a U.S. Navy destroyer was made invisible and teleported from Philadelphia, Pennsylvania, to Norfolk, Virginia. Records in the Archives Branch of the Naval History and Heritage Command have been repeatedly searched, but no documents have been located which confirm the event, or any interest by the Navy in attempting such an achievement. Why would there be any evidence of this disaster when our government and military have been known to experiment on U.S. citizens and military without their knowledge? The ship involved in the experiment was the *USS Eldridge*.

Supposedly, the crew of the civilian merchant ship *SS Andrew Furuseth* observed the arrival via teleportation of the *Eldridge* into the Norfolk area. Some went insane. Others developed mysterious illnesses. But others still were said to have been fused together with the ship; still alive, but with their limbs sealed to the metal.

ET stories have shown abductees the future, can move through walls and other solid objects. There are many portals located around the Earth. There is one in the Mexico/Central America area, one in the Sinai, one in Tibet, another one in Easter Island, Mount Fiji, Mount Shasta, Lake Titicaca, the Nazca lines, Ulura, and in the Bermuda triangle region. There are more where people have stepped into other dimensions and times.

You see we are in the infancy of opening the secrets to our world and the Universe. Time does not exist as we know it. The past, present, and future exist simultaneously. When you get the feeling of Déjà vu, you jumped into the future for a moment.

Waiting to be Saved

In my last predictions book, *2020 Prophecies and Predictions,* I wrote that I don't foresee any outside aid coming from angelic or advanced beings to save us from COVID. There are benevolent beings out there, but I believe there is a "noninterference law" that they can't get involved, not unless there's a huge threat to the planet with a nuclear launch.

If there is a non-interference law, it must be on a case by case bases. People have reported being instantly healed by aliens, but also harmed or killed by the aliens. Some people have simply vanished never to be seen again. There are stories of nuclear missile tests that were suddenly shut down or malfunctioned due to a UFO or UFOs hovering over the military launch area. Every abduction case is different.

Many energies from other worlds and dimensions are coming into Earth's energy field to participate in this great moment in time. That's why the increased UFO sightings in the past year. The benevolent beings want us to awaken to who were once were as beings of Light when we first arrived on this planet millions of years ago.

Expect more sightings of bizarre cloud formations, orbs, and UFO in 2021. Remember, UFOs can shape-shift into whatever form they want—helicopters, planes, and especially clouds.

Recently, hundreds of UFOs were captured by the International Space Station and the video was posted on YouTube. There's going to be a mass landing in the very near future and the military and the world's governments can't deny or debunk their existence.

Holographic Inserts

Holographic inserts have been used for a long time to control consciousness and to change the story of information to one of disinformation, especially with the younger generation. Those who use the holographic inserts are not always beings of light or upliftment. There are dark ulterior motives afoot. Just like our movie industry has influenced humanity, there are those in space who have a holographic industry and influence us. They have been around for thousands of years and they have found how easily we are fooled by their technology. What is real and what is Memorex (remember the commercial)?

Humans have engineered holographic inserts as well and they can create many dramas and illusions for us. Just pull back the curtain and you will see the real Wizard of Oz. In 2008, Elvis Presley joined Celine Dion for a duet, "If I Can Dream" on American Idol—but Elvis wasn't real. He was a great example of holographic technology. The video is still on YouTube and it will give you chills, it's so lifelike!

Holographic inserts look exactly like 3-D reality, and it will be extremely hard to tell the difference. Some of the huge events will be real and others will be inserts designed to move humanity toward the "One World Order" of control. Some of the inserts have been used in ancient times to project religious stories around the world.

How will you know what is real and what is holographic? It takes a lot of energy to create holographic images, so the vibration is different. Some of the alien abductions and different aliens could actually be holographic inserts—whatever they want us to believe. The only difference between reality and holographic inserts is that the holographic inserts vibrate at an incredible rate.

What alarms me are the stories of cloned humans being dumped off on Native American reservations by alien craft and taken to cities. What is their purpose—to observe or interact with us? Are they programmed to harm us or create havoc in cities? Only time will tell what their true agenda might be.

The Star Children

Already Star Children are entering our world and they know their mission having been instructed by higher spiritual beings before their birth. That's why the new Star Children must be given education instructions to guide them with their extraordinary extrasensory talents. These children will have psychic and telekinetic abilities and see into other worlds. Don't be surprised if your child or grandchild tells you about Star Beings! I described them to my parents at the age of three.

ETs are contacting children worldwide. UFOs have been observed landing near schools and ETs leaving the craft. One such story was included in this book that took place at Ariel Elementary School in Ruwa, Zimbabwe on September 16, 1994, where 62 children witnessed a UFO land and alien beings exit the craft. On February 4, 1977, fourteen students at Broad Haven Elementary School in Haverfordwest, South Wales watched a landed UFO and

ET emerge from the craft. On March 21, 1966, eighty-seven students at Hillsdale College in Hillsdale, Michigan observed a UFO land in front of their school.

Humanity is learning a great lesson at this time. The lesson is to stop being victims to the Family of Dark and to realize our godliness, our connectedness with Prime Creator, and with all that exists through the never-ending Cosmos—both the good and bad, and the darkness and the light. We are connected to everything! Some of you may think this is "new age" malarkey, but I can assure you that there are higher spiritual beings that care and love us. We are magnificent beings, members of the Family of Light, and we came to Earth at this time to create a shift and assist in the transition. We volunteered for this assignment and this challenging time. Many will pass at this time to watch the major events unfolding on Earth while others remain to experience the great shift.

There are 7.8 billion souls on this planet now. What are these people thinking right now—fear, hate, and anger? That much energy is alive on Earth. Can you imagine if humanity came together to create the *Butterfly in the Hurricane* moment in time, shifting the dark control into planetary Light? Remember how you once believed in Santa Claus and the Easter Bunny and then one day your beliefs were shattered when your parents told you they weren't real. But this time you will find out that aliens do exist, and they are here on Earth and they have been here for eons. You will discover that there has been a massive cover-up to keep us victims.

Consider the huge angels the Russian Cosmonauts encountered during their space mission. Do you think there were hallucinating? The Cosmos is full of diverse lifeforms, like the stars in the sky!

There is connectedness and purpose in all things—the many histories for the Earth, the galactic history, and the universal history.

The stories in this book are only a few of the incredible things that have and are taking place on our planet's surface, below the surface in deep subterranean bases, and the deepest regions of our oceans. Life is complex and has evolved for billions and billions of years on dimensional worlds, galaxies, and universes that we can't even fathom. We are not unique!

Visions of the Future

History seems to repeat itself. In another 100 years, there will be another virus, just as deadly or deadlier than COVID-19. Most of us living today, except for our children and their children will be alive to see that.

I foresee the White House will be moved from Washington, D.C. to Nebraska after a disaster of some kind before the year 2035. It might be a nuclear or natural disaster—like a major earthquake. A huge earthquake is not out of the question. On August 23, 2011, a magnitude 5.8 earthquake struck at 1:51 p.m. only 90 miles southwest of Washington, D.C.

2021 Looking into The Future

AFTERWORD

BLACK ELK'S VISIONS

Today, November 11, 2020, I received a message from a Facebook friend who described her lucid dream. In the dream, she saw a blue man shrinking in size, and a light bulb went off in my head—I then understood more of Black Elk's remarkable visions of the future.

In *Mother Earth Spirituality,* my mentor Oglala Sioux Ceremonial Leader Ed McGaa "Eagle Man" (1936-2017) gave his interpretation of Black Elk's visions for us and our planet. "Visions and foretelling prophecies are not uncommon among my people, the Oglala," Ed wrote. "The demanding Vision Quest—in which the seeker stays alone, on an isolated mountain top or badlands butte— the Sun Dance ritual and the powerful Yuwipi (Spirit-calling) Ceremony, have resulted in strong foretelling power for our holy men and holy women.

Black Elk (1863-1950), also known as *Hehaka Sapa* and

Nicholas Black Elk, was a famous holy man, traditional healer, and visionary of the Oglala Lakota (Sioux) of the northern Great Plains. He was born in December of 1863 on the Little Powder River in Wyoming, west of present-day South Dakota. He was the son of the elder Black Elk, who supported Chief Crazy Horse, the Lakota resistance leader, and White Cow Sees Woman. He had five sisters and one brother.

Black Elk was born December 1, in the sun sign of Sagittarius, an astrological sign linked to seers and prophets like Nostradamus, born December 14, 1863. During Black Elk's lifetime, he witnessed many battles: he was three-years-old when the Fetterman Battle took place in 1866, he was five-years-old during the signing of the 1868 Fort Laramie Treaty, and about 12 years old when the Battle of the Little Big Horn was fought, and General George A. Custer and his soldier perished. He experienced the end of the Sioux wars and the beginning of aggressive federal "Pacification" policies imposed by the U.S. government upon his people.

In 1877, the Lakota people, including Black Elk and his family, fled north into Canada. They followed Chief Sitting Bull, who had become the Lakota resistance leader after the stabbing death of Crazy Horse. Following Chief Sitting bull's surrender and arrest, Black Elk, his family, and other Lakota returned to internment on the Pine Ridge Reservation.

In 1886, Black Elk rejoined Buffalo Bill Cody's Wild West Show. He traveled with the show throughout the United States and Europe. When he finally returned home to the Pine Ridge Reservation, he became their spiritual authority and supported the Ghost Dance movement, based on the belief that the dance would cause white people to leave and the buffalo to return to them, which had been nearly killed to extinction by white soldiers and pioneers. Black Elk was a witness to the Wounded Knee Massacre on December 29, 1890, near Wounded Knee Creek on the Lakota Pine Ridge Indian Reservation in the U.S. state of South Dakota.

According to some eye-witnesses, the U.S. 7th Cavalry Regiment commanded by Major Samuel M. Whiteside intercepted Spotted Elk's band of Miniconjou Lakota and 38 Hunkpapa Lakota near Porcupine Butte and escorted them 5 miles westward to Wound Knee Creek, where they made camp. On December 29, troops went to disarm the Lakota, and one version of the story claimed an Indian rifle accidentally discharged causing the 7th Cavalry to open fire from all sides, killing men, women, and children, as well as some of their own fellow soldiers. By the time the gunfire ended more than 200 men, women, and children of the Lakota tribe were dead and 51 were wounded (4 men, 47 women, and children, some of whom died later). Twenty-five soldiers also died that day and 39 were wounded. At least twenty soldiers were awarded the Medal of Honor, but in 2001, the National Congress of American Indians passed two resolutions condemning the awards and called on the U.S. government to rescind the. The site of the battlefield has been designated as a National Historic Landmark.

It is said that Black Elk, on horseback, charged the soldiers and helped to rescue some of the wounded. A bullet grazed his hip.

In 1931, author John G. Neihardt interviewed Black Elk at age 68 about his life and visions in a book titled, *Black Elk Speaks*, published in 1932. Black Elk spoke of a new world.

Black Elk was nine years old when he became very ill and was unresponsive for several days. During this time, he had a powerful vision in which he was visited by the Thunder Beings (Wakinyan), and taken to the Grandfathers—spiritual representatives of the six sacred directions: west, east, north, south, above, and below.

These "spirits were represented as kind and loving, full of years and wisdom, like revered human grandfathers." When he was seventeen, Black Elk told a medicine man, Black Road, about the vision in detail. Black Road and the other medicine men of the village were "astonished by the greatness of the vision."

Part of Black Elk's vision involved the Earth becoming sick as we are experiencing in the twenty-first century. The animals, the winged ones, and the four-legged ones grew frightened and all living things became poor and sickly. The air and the waters dirtied and smelled foul. And then Black Elk saw a blue man creating the sickness on Mother Earth. The powers of the four directions, represented by four horses, charged the blue man but were beaten back. Then the Grandfathers called upon Black Elk who picked up his bow which transformed into a spear. He swooped down on the blue man, killing him. After the blue man was dead, all life came back upon the Earth; all things fresh and healed again.

The blue man represents the Family of Dark and their agenda for the earth—their greed and hunger for power and domination over the Earth.

A red man appeared among the people. His transformation into a buffalo indicated a time of plenty. A sacred herb became four flowers, four blossoms on a single stem. The four-rayed herb—red, yellow, black, and white, became the flowering tree. Black Elk heard a song: A good nation I will make live, this nation above has said, they have given me the power to makeover.

Then Black Elk saw the sacred hoop of his people was only one of many hoops, all joined together to make one great circle, the great hoop of all peoples. In the center of the great hoop stood a powerful, shelter, flowering tree, and under it gathered children of all nations.

At the end of Black Elk's vision, two-spirit men gave him the day-break-star herb of understanding. He dropped the herb down to the world below, and it flowered, spreading its power out into the whole world. In time, he was promised his people would be free and would help spread this power of peace and understanding.

Black Elk lived to be an old man—dying at age 87. In his lifetime he witnessed the free spirit of the mystic warriors of the plains become a tethered eagle to a *washichu's*, or white man's, zoo. He and his people became captives of the dark reservation road. Old warriors waited in remoteness, amid poverty and despair, for the promise of yesterday.

In Dr. Ardy Sixkiller Clarke's book, *Encounters with Star People,* she was told a story about Black Elk and a special stone he carried with him all his life after a UFO encounter. The story goes that Black Elk was visiting his cousin Benjamin. He was in the sweat lodge, when according to Benjamin's family; a circular craft came out of the sky and hovered over it. Suddenly a stone penetrated the closed door and landed between Black Elk's feet. He picked up the stone but had to complete the sweat lodge ceremony before he could leave. By the time he was able to leave the lodge, the spacecraft was gone. Another holy man on the reservation remembered Black Elk and how he carried the rock and how he still used the sacred pipe. He said that when he lit his sacred pipe, Black Elk would laugh and call his pipe an antenna for contacting the Star People.

Dr. Clarke's source said, "Black Elk believed the Star People came to Earth hundreds of thousands of years ago from Sirius and the Pleiades. He called them the answers of the people."

From what I've heard indigenous people worldwide have communicated with Star People for eons and continue to connect with them. In Dr. Clarke's travels to South America and speaking to the Maya people, she was told that the Star People have warned them that we are going from the Fourth World into the Fifth World where a great cleansing will take place. The Maya have no fear of these Earth changes because they know how to survive in the natural world unlike people in the Western world who live the cities and have no idea how to survive in nature.

I agree with Ed McGaa that the blue man of Black Elk's vision is symbolic of all those who harm Mother Earth and her creatures and do so knowingly. The blue man, the great violator, symbolizes greed, corruption, dishonesty, and selfishness. Mother Earth, represented by the four directions, has fought back against the one who has made the grass and animals sick and the streams and air unclean. Mother Earth has natural self-healing powers, but without the help of knowledgeable humans, she cannot set herself right. A reversal of the world values, a spiritual concept of the Earth as God-created and sacred, is in order before we two-leggeds can be environmentally effective on a global basis. The blue man will meet his death when takes place.

Ed said this, "Brothers and sisters, we must go back to some of the old ways if we are going to truly save our Mother Earth and bring back the natural beauty that every person seriously needs, especially in this day of vanishing species, vanishing rain forests, overpopulation, poisoned waters, acid rain, a thinning ozone layer, drought, rising temperatures, and weapons of complete annihilation. In conclusion, our survival is dependent on the realization that Mother Earth is a truly holy (conscious) being, that all things in the world are holy and must not be violated, and that we must share and be generous with one another. Think of your fellow men and women as holy people who were put here by the Great Spirit. Think of being related to all things!"

This is a Cree Indian saying, *There will come a time when the birds will fall from the trees, the rivers will be poisoned, and the wolves will die in the forests. But then the warriors of the rainbow will appear and save the world.*

We are seeing a great disparity between the Democrats and the Republicans never seen before. And it goes beyond politics. We are at the crossroads of change, but will that change be violent or peaceful. We say that "history repeats itself." In mass consciousness, we have believed that saying and created a continuation of the same experiences.

A massive awakening is taking place on our planet. Events are quickening and unfolding and seeping into everyone's reality. We are experiencing in 2020, the master number 22 energy. It brings with it karmic lessons and master teachings. The Earth is moving into a higher vibration and those who remain in the lower vibration levels will not survive the coming changes.

Some of you have ignored or ridicules the ancient prophecies but they are coming to fruition. This is not a time to become a shrinking violet. You, as a System Buster, will show the way in times when people are desperate because the old ways are no longer solutions—they no longer fit and no longer apply.

Life the best that you can each day and be a shining example for the new generations. As you raise your vibratory rates, you become your light body. Stop listening to the major news that who embellish events for better ratings. Those of you who are Light carriers will come into questions in the next few years. This is part of the plan. Say this each day, *"It is my intention that I be safe always in all things that I do. It is my intention that I receive love and give love in all things that I do. It is my intention that I never fear the changes around me. It is my intention that I will not become overly enamored of the material world."* Change is inevitable—it's how to respond to it that will transform our world.

As we have been told, live in the moment and to stop living in the future. It's time to stop worrying about "what if" scenarios—the future is still forming, and mass consciousness is creating it!

2021 Looking into The Future

BIBLIOGRAPHY

Ball, Marshall Stewart, *Kiss of God: The Wisdom of a Silent Child*, Health Communications, Inc., Deerfield Beach, Florida, 1990.

Clarke, Dr. Ardy Sixkiller, *Encounters with Star People*, and *Sky People*, Anomalist Books, San Antonio, TX 78209

David, Gary A., *Star Shines and Earthworks of the Desert Southwest*, 2012, Adventures Unlimited Press

Fowler, Raymond, *The Andreasson Affair,* Englewood: Prentice Hall, 1982, *The Watchers, New York:* Bantam Books, 1990, *The Watchers II, Newberg, OR*: Wild Flower Press, 1995.

Harney, Corbin, *The Way It Is,* Blue Dolphin Publishing, *Nevada City, Nevada, 1995.*

McGaa, Ed, *Spirituality for America: Earth-Saving Wisdom for the Indigenous:* 2013 and Mother Earth Spirituality, Harper San Francisco, *San Francisco, CA*, 1990.

Sunbow, *The Sasquatch Message to Humanity: Conversations with Elder Kamooh,* Comanche Spirit Publishing, 2016.

2021 Looking into The Future

ABOUT THE AUTHOR

Author, International Clairvoyant, and Earth Mysteries investigator Betsey Lewis had her first UFO encounter at the age of 8 months of age with her parents who were driving from Northwest Idaho to Southern Idaho late one night. Years later, a family member recalled her parents had lost two hours in time during their trip. In 1982, Betsey and her mother were hypnotized by MUFON investigator and author Ann Druffel and take back to that night in Idaho. Betsey and her mother revealed an abduction by gray aliens. At age seven, Betsey had a UFO encounter walking home from her elementary school in Idaho. Shortly after the event, she was shown future catastrophic Earth changes in recurring dreams.

For the past forty years, Betsey has investigated alien stories, UFOs sightings, ancient archaeological sites in Louisiana and Belize, and Native American petroglyph sites throughout the Northwest. She conducted field investigations into the bizarre cattle mutilations throughout the Northwest during the late 1970s and early 1980s, collaborating with renowned cattle mutilation investigator Tom Adams to uncover the cattle mutilation mystery.

In the 1990s, Betsey was mentored by two well-known Native American spiritual leaders—Western Shoshone Nation leader and author Corbin Harney and Ed McGaa "Eagle Man, an Oglala Sioux Ceremonial Leader, and author.

Betsey has been a frequent guest on Coast to Coast AM since 2013, Ground Zero with Clyde Lewis, KTALK's The Fringe Paranormal Show, Fade to Black, WGSO AM radio in New Orleans, Paranormal Central, and other well-known radio shows. She was a keynote speaker at the Alamo/Las Vegas UFO Conference in 2013 and speaker at the UFO Conference in Albuquerque, New Mexico in 2017.

Betsey's writing inspiration came from her talented step-uncle William "Bill" Peter Blatty (1928-2017), director, screenplay writer, producer, and author of the New York best-selling novel *The Exorcist*.

To learn more about Betsey, her non-fiction and children's books, her upcoming Events, Newsletters, and daily Earth News blog, visit **www.betseylewis.com**

2021 Looking into The Future

Printed in Great Britain
by Amazon